Who Killed Tammy Jo?

Olivia Watson

Published by Trellis Publishing, 2021.

WHO KILLED TAMMY JO?

First edition. July 2, 2021.

Copyright © 2021 Olivia Watson.

ISBN: 979-8224825417

Written by Olivia Watson.

WHO KILLED TAMMY JO

Olivia Watson

Chapter 1

It was a cold, wet morning on November 10, 1979. It had rained nonstop the night before. The dark clouds had cleared seemingly to allow the morning sun to wake up the farmers in Caledonia, a rural area about a half hour's drive from Rochester, New York.

Although he didn't know it at the time, this day would be one that stuck with Wes Clements the rest of his life.

Wes Clements was around ten years old in 1979. He and his father lived and worked on a farm in Caledonia and had risen with the sun that day, happy to see it after a long stretch of rainy weather. The pair was getting ready to go over their cornfields with the ol' combine tractor that morning, but their plans got delayed when they made a startling discovery.

Just inside the borders of their cornfields, the part of their fields that backed up on a nearby freeway, was the body of a teenage girl face down.

"We didn't know at first that it was a dead girl," Clements has said. "We thought it might be some kind of Halloween prank gone wrong, like a balloon that had floated away or something."

In fact, it was the body of Tammy Jo Alexander, but Clements wouldn't know that until over 35 years. At the time, she was just the girl in the cornfield.

The girl in the Clements's cornfield looked like a young teenager. She was petite, about 5 feet 3 inches tall and 120 pounds. She had brown eyes and light brown hair that was bleach blonde at the ends. Her hair was wavy and was just long enough to dust her shoulders.

The girl's skin was tan, she had visible tan lines from a halter top and her face and shoulders were speckled with freckles and acne. She was cute, but not quite old enough to be beautiful yet. She had had plenty more growing still to do before her life was cut recklessly short.

The Clements's also couldn't help but notice the girl's clothing. She was dressed fairly typical for a girl her age—she was wearing a plaid button-up shirt and tan corduroy pants—but her jacket was seemingly unique. It was a man's nylon-lined, red windbreaker jacket with thick, stark black lines running down the arms. Later, a label inside the coat was found marking it as manufactured by *Auto Sports Products Inc.*

Along with typical clothing, the young girl was also wearing jewelry. She had a silver necklace with three small turquoise stones around her neck and two silver keychains attached to her belt loops. The first was shaped like a heart and read *He who holds the key can open my heart.* The other was the key, made to fit a cutout on its heart-shaped companion.

When Wes Clements and his father Harry realized what they were looking at, they immediately called police.

The first responder on the scene was John York of the Caledonia Police Department.

"I was not far away. I arrived on the scene with Harry and his son as we walked to the area where the body was found," said Officer York. "She was laying face down in a cornfield. Somewhat off the road, about 20 yards laying in the corn."

It seems silly to dump a murder victim so close to a popular freeway on paper, but in reality it was almost impossible to see the spot she was left for dead from the road. Corn stalks are tall and grow thickly. The dense vegetation is difficult to see through. Officer York himself needed guidance from Harry Clements and his young son Wes to navigate through the crop to the body.

When Officer York first laid eyes on the girl he thought she may have been the victim of a hit-and-run accident. Maybe a trucker was going a bit too fast and didn't see the girl crossing the road until it was too late. It made sense. However, when he got closer to the body he saw two distinctive gunshot wounds—one on her head and the other on her back. She had been shot than left for dead in the cornfield.

"We secured the area and began an investigation that we thought would be very normal," says Officer York. "But it became anything but a normal homicide investigation."

The young girl had no identification on her, her pockets had been turned inside-out seemingly by her assailant, so she was officially declared a Jane Doe. As her case continued and her identity remained a secret she took to the grave with her, she became known more specifically as Cali Doe after the area she was found in.

Chapter 2

The investigation into Cali Doe's death had the odds stacked against it from the beginning.

First, there was the rain. Caledonia had been soaked by heavy rains that fell consistently for days before the discovery of Cali Doe's body. The whole crime scene and surrounding area was soaking wet, saturated with rain.

Second, there was the location. Caledonia was a small community, but one on the road to bigger places. The freeway that ran through the town and right next to where Cali Doe was found was the 520, a major truck route that connected Canada to the US. Across the road from the farm was also a heavily treed pull-off area where a lot of trucks were known to stop and rest.

Third, there was the fact that she had no identification.

All three of these factors had a major effect on the case. The rain meant that any physical evidence around Cali Doe's body had been either degraded, destroyed, or washed away. The location made it difficult because it indicated that a truck driver may have been involved, meaning that the perpetrator would be from out of town and not known by the locals. The lack of identification meant that investigators had nowhere to start.

In the face of all this hardship though, Officer York stayed positive and focused on what little evidence he did have to work with. He became the lead investigator on the case and stuck with it for decades, even after

Officer York was intrigued by the fact that Cali Doe's skin was so tan. She had had the marks of a halter top or bikini engraved into her skin by the sun. Especially in the face of all the rain Caledonia had gotten lately, the recent tan mean that Cali Doe was probably from a sunnier part of the country—that or she'd just got back from vacation.

Initially, Officer York thought that he would find a missing person's report matching Cali Doe's description when he began looking in the larger area of Livingston County but he never did.

"We thought if we looked in Livingston County we would get an identification the next morning," said Officer York. "If we put it on the television, someone would pick up the phone and someone would say I know that girl."

No such phone call ever came.

Wes Clements and his father Harry, who had discovered Cali Doe's body on their farm, were quickly cleared from the case. They were questioned separately and provided matching accounts of their morning and night before. The father and son also willingly provided shoeprint samples and other forms of forensic samples when requested.

Little physical evidence was found where Cali Doe's body had been left in the cornfield, but more evidence was found in the surrounding area. After the coroner's report revealed that Cali Doe had been shot in the back in the spot she was found, but she had first been shot in the head somewhere else.

Investigators tried to recreate Cali Doe's pathway through the cornfield to the road and found an area along the roadside that appeared to be stained with blood. Cali Doe had been shot in the head unaware on the side of the freeway and then dragged into the field where she was shot in the back once more for good measure.

Investigators tried to search the surrounding cornfield and areas along the freeway to find more evidence such as a discarded ID card or purse contents but retrieved nothing.

The coroner's report revealed a few other clues about the identity and last day of Cali Doe's life such as the girl's last meal. Within an hour of being killed, Cali Doe had eaten a simple meal of corn, potatoes, and boiled ham. Eatery food. It filled you up, but it wasn't fancy.

It hurt Cali Doe to chew her final meal. A molar on her left side seemed to have had a cavity for over a year and one on the right was even worse. To have either fixed would've meant the first trip to the dentist for the sixteen-year-old.

While her last meal seems like inconsequential evidence, it lead to one of the most important discoveries in the early days of the Cali Doe investigation. It lead Officer York and his team to Marge Bradford, a waitress at the Lima Diner 25 minutes down the road from the Clements's cornfield.

Chapter 3

After the coroner assigned to Cali Doe's case revealed that the young girl had eaten a typical diner meal of corn, potatoes, and boiled ham within an hour of being killed, Officer York was struck with an idea.

"We wanted to find something or someone who had seen Cali Doe right before she ended up in the cornfield. I assigned investigators to then drive down the road and visit every rest stop and restaurant they ran into." Said Officer York.

Officer York and his team visited over 70 restaurants. Eventually, they came across the Lima Diner, which was nestled into nearby Lima's downtown—an intersection dubbed by locals as *The Four Corners*.

In 1979 Marge Bradford was a waitress at the Lima Diner. She was 21-years-old and lived in a trailer down the street, close enough for her to walk to work.

On November 11, 1979, Bradford met Officer York and his team when she arrived to work around 2pm. They asked her if she had seen anyone matching Cali Doe's description two nights earlier and astonishingly, she had.

November 9 was a Friday, and every Friday night at the Lima Diner was fish fry night. At about 8:30pm, two people walked into the restaurant and sat in Bradford's section.

"I'd never seen them before. They were strangers," Bradford told the officers. "On Friday nights you usually got the regulars, you know, always the same people for fish fry night. Most of them were my friends."

But these two weren't. The pair had arrived in the restaurant fairly late for a fish fry night, which was a busy time for the small diner. By the time Cali Doe and her mystery companion walked into the restaurant almost all the locals had cleared out since the dinner rush, but it was still too early for the bar crowd to start shuffling in. They were just about the only two people in the restaurant besides staff at the time.

According to Bradford, Cali Doe's companion was a man around 25-years-old, was around six feet tall, and had light brown curly hair and glasses.

"They seemed know each other but didn't seem like they were boyfriend and girlfriend. More like brother and sister or something like that," Bradford said. "That was the impression I got."

Bradford told police that there didn't seem to be anything unusual about the two's time in the diner. The young girl matching Cali Doe's description seemed happy, she didn't seem nervous or upset about anything. She in fact spent most of the time laughing with her companion.

Nothing about the pair struck a chord of worry in Bradford or any of the other staff, which in itself is one of the strangest aspects of the case. Cali Doe was found murdered only eight-and-a-half miles up the freeway.

"Why would you buy someone dinner and kill them 25 minutes later and throw them in a cornfield? I had never made any sense to me. She didn't act worried at all. Or afraid." Said Bradford.

Investigators worked with Bradford to draw up a composite sketch of the man seen with Cali Doe and the sketch was spread all around the county but it never lead to a suspect. They remained confident that Bradford had seen the actual Cali Doe though as Bradford had been able to describe her distinctive jacket in detail. She also described the meal she served to the young girl that night—it had been a simple meal of corn, potatoes, and boiled ham.

Chapter 4

After Marge Bradford, a waitress at the Lima Diner, was able to prove she had seen Cali Doe alive and well and with a companion within an hour of her death, investigators and lead officer John York were confident they were now on the right path to discovery who Cali Doe was as well as how she ended up dead in a cornfield. They were wrong.

Bradford's description of Cali Doe's companion turned up no new leads, and the diner provided them with no new information about Cali Doe except for the direction she had been travelling in. The case began to lose heat quickly, investigators had nowhere to go with the case.

"Typically within a week somebody's called. A friend, a family member, somebody has reported her missing and launch the missing person report. But a week went by, months went by, nothing." Said Officer York.

So Officer York began searching in new places, and remained the primary detective on the case for decades to come despite being promoted to the Livingston County Sheriff's department in 1989. No one worked harder on the case than York, who had felt the weight of the young girl's case since he was first led into the Clements's cornfield.

"The investigation began for me in November 1979 and continued for 36 years," said now Sheriff York. "You like to take pride in your work and think you're going to get resolve and justice for every victim. It's not realistic but you believe that. My personal belief was that Cali Doe had the right to better. She deserved better."

The more the years passed, the more York wanted answers for the young girl. He began to take the case personally, as it soon became the only unsolved case he had ever worked on. He became obsessed.

York spent months alone trying to dig up information on Cali Doe's distinctive jacket. It didn't look like it belonged to her, so he was hoping it could've been her killer's. Plus, it looked different than any jacket you could buy in a typical department store. It looked unique, unique enough to lead directly to one individual person—or so York hoped.

York spent weeks trying to locate the jacket's manufacturer, *Auto Sports Products Inc.*, which was named in the jacket's tag. He sent photos of the jacket along with the company's name to the FBI and received no response. He wrote letters to every State Senator in the country as well. One Senator recognized the label, and replied to York. The manufacturer was a mushroom farmer in California.

Again, York was initially hopeful but couldn't be for too long. The mushroom farmer, as it turned out, had been the Vice President of a major car manufacturer in the late '70s. He had made several thousands of the coats, which were given away to auto sports companies and other car manufacturers as a promotional item. There was no way to tell where the coats had been sent and who had received them. It was another dead end.

York remained ever determined, but he now began to scramble. He had artist renderings of Cali Doe made from autopsy photos and sent them all over the country along with the sketch of her companion from the night she was killed. He took the story international to Mexico, and began personally talking to police departments across the country, begging them to double check their missing persons and runaway reports. Nothing pertinent ever came up.

In the late 1970's hitchhiking was fairly common and sadly so was occurences of hitchhikers becoming vulnerable targets for predators. That's why York decided he had to consider that Cali Doe had been killed by the worst of the worst—a serial killer. He wanted to talk to some serial killers that had modus operandis that matched the evidence in the Cali Doe case. One of those men were Henry Lee Lucas.

Henry Lee Lucas was a serial killer from Waco, Texas who liked to confess to murders he didn't commit—many of which remain attributed to him today. Officer York decided to interview Lucas in 1984. Lucas, in his normal style, confessed to the crime but was unable to provide any new facts about the murder and got several facts about the murder incorrect during his confession to York, including the colour of Cali Doe's distinctive jacket.

After talking to Lucas, York was convinced he had played no role in the murder and crossed the serial killer off his list of suspects. Ottis Toole, another serial killer who was a friend of Henry Lee Lucas's, was also interviewed by York. Although Toole's description of events matched the story Lucas had given York, he was also ruled out as a suspect. York believes that both men got what little information they did know about the case from newspapers and the TV as the case was widely publicized across the nation thanks to York's efforts.

Although York refused to give up on the case, it would be over 20 years before any new information emerged.

Chapter 5

In September of 2005, Cali Doe's body was exhumed in order to have DNA samples collected. The hope was she could eventually be identified through a DNA match with any living relatives. It had been 26 years since the young girl's body was found in the cornfield and countless advances in forensic science and investigation practices had been made. Cali Doe's DNA was automatically ran through CODIS, the Combined DNA Index System used by the FBI, on the off chance one of her family members were in the system but unsurprisingly a match was not found.

Cali Doe's DNA was collected by the University of North Texas Center for Human Identification. Despite Cali Doe being buried for almost three decades, they were able to produce a mitochondrial DNA profile for the girl through DNA profiling.

While her body was consumed, Cali Doe also had several of her teeth removed, which were then sent for mineralogical and forensic isotope analysis. This was done because investigators still had no idea where the young girl was from. Luckily, tap water across the US varies in quality because every area of the US has different mineral compositions and combinations. When you drink the water in your own area, the specific mineral compositions leave markers in your bones and teeth as they develop. Using this modern forensic science, investigators were able to prove for the first time that Cali Doe was definitively from the Southern region of the US.

This evidence was strengthened in 2006 when forensic palynology was conducted on Cali Doe's clothing. This meant that pollen from her clothing was collected, analyzed, and matched with an area in the US that contained all samples. If an area of the US could be found, that would likely be the area that Cali Doe was from.

The pollen found on Cali Doe's clothing was determined in 2006, and again in 2012, to have originated from California, Arizona, or Florida.Amazingly, nine years after the pollen was first analyzed, the palynology findings would be proven correct when Cali Doe was positively identified in 2015.

Chapter 6

Facebook has been one of the most defining elements of the 2000's since it was made available to the world in 2006. In a very strange way, it also helped uncover the true identity of Cali Doe.

In 2015, a woman that had gone to school with Cali Doe began perusing the social media website looking for old classmates. While she was able to find an account for most of her old friends, she failed to find one for one of her favorite friends from high school, Tammy Jo Alexander.

Tammy Jo Alexander and the woman had attended high school together in Brooksville, Florida. After the summer of '79 Alexander never came back to school, and no one ever really knew why beyond rumours. While she couldn't find any trace of Tammy Jo Alexander on the internet, Alexander's classmate was able to track down Alexander's half-sister Pamela Dyson, who now lived in Panama City.

Dyson wasn't able to provide much information about Alexander's current whereabouts. Alexander had worked as a waitress in a truck stop and had a habit of running away. She liked to hitchhike and would often catch rides with the men she met in the truck stop. One summer, she took a ride to California on a whim with her best friend. She loved travelling and told her folks upon her return that she planned to do it again.

Dyson knew her sister had gone missing in 1979, but her home life at the time left her in the dark about any developments in the case. Alexander and Dyson's mother had been a violent alcoholic who was addicted to prescription drugs and often lashed out at the girls. It was a volatile environment and both young girls did everything they could to avoid confrontations. When Alexander disappeared, Dyson quickly learned that it was not to be spoken about.

But Dyson did believe that her mother had filed a missing persons report so Dyson went with Alexander's classmate to the Hernando County sheriff's office to check in on the report. When they arrived, there was no report on file. It is likely that Alexander's mom wasn't taken seriously when filing the report as Alexander had a history of running away.

Up to this point in her life, Dyson had believed that Tammy Jo Alexander had walked away from her volatile home life to start fresh somewhere else. She pictured her in California, living by the beach with a husband and children. It would've been a loving household, as Alexander remained happy and bright-spirited despite living in a volatile hell.

When Dyson found out no one had looked into what had happened to her sister back in the late 70's she became very worried—the idyllic image she had had of her half-sister crumbled to pieces. She decided to file her own missing persons report. Tammy Jo Alexander was officially listed as missing, and her file was posted into the National Missing and Unidentified Persons System, or NamUs. NamUs is used across America to identify Jane and John Does and to make missing persons information available nationwide.

Along with basic information about her sister and their life, Dyson included an old school photo of Alexander from the year before she went missing. Shortly after Alexander's missing persons profile was entered into NamUs, her photo was recognized by an unbelievable source.

Carl Koppelman was a Californian artist who had spent his life creating artistic reconstructions from unidentified corpses. Officer York had gotten Koppelman to create a reconstruction of Cali Doe both in 2010 and 2014. A year since his last reconstruction of the young girl, he was now positive he was staring at her real face and her real name.

Koppelman immediately emailed the Livingston County sheriff's office, which was still overseeing the Cali Doe case 36 years later even though John York had retired in 2013. The resemblance was confirmed after Dyson's DNA was compared to Cali Doe's taken in 2005. The results were clear—the two women shared the same mother.

Cali Doe was finally identified as Tammy Jo Alexander.

John York, the primary detective on Cali Doe's case for 34 years found the identification to be bittersweet. He was relieved to know that Tammy Jo Alexander wouldn't have to rest unnamed any longer, but it was a stark reminder that they still didn't know who her killer was. The identification of Cali Doe as Tammy Jo Alexander did not bring in any new viable leads, although the as of January of 2017 the case remains classified as active.

Cali Doe had been buried in the Dansville Cemetery in Dansville, New York since her autopsy. Her grave had been marked by a donated headstone inscripted with the name Caledonia Jane Doe and an approximated lifespan.

After Tammy Jo Alexander's identification, Dyson decided to keep her sister buried in peace where she had been for so many years. A proper funeral service was finally conducted for the young woman and a nearby funeral home paid to have the headstone replaced with another that told the true story of the young girl's life.

Tammy Jo Alexander's death was both tragic and uplifting. It is always tragic when a young life is taken in a brutal way, especially when they remain nameless for decades after, but it is equally uplifting to see a community embrace a victim who had no one else to stand up for her. The community in Livingston County and Officer John York made sure Cali Doe was never forgotten. And for their efforts, a family and many friends now know what happened to the bright, beautiful, and bubbly Tammy Jo Alexander.

AMBER Alert: The Murder of Amber Creek

RENEE DUCKWORTH

Amber Gail Creek, who preferred to be called 'Aimee', was born on July 2, 1982 in Park Ridge, Cook County, Illinois. Her parents had lived together for just two years and had never married by the time that they each went their separate ways. Amber lived with her mother, Elizabeth Mowers, in the village of Lake Zurich, a north-western residential suburb of Chicago, until she was six years old. This was far from a happy home. Her mother was a cocaine addict who would often use in front of her daughter. Amber also divulged that a man had sexually abused her whilst she was under her mother's care. The Illinois Department of Children and Family Services stepped in and Amber's father Robert Creek was awarded sole custody of his daughter. She was sent to live with him in the nearby suburb of Palatine.

It was here that Amber grew up. Contact between Amber and her mother was all but cut off. Initially she was haunted by memories of the abuse and would often cry herself to sleep at night. However, over time, and despite the abuse, separation of her parents and the shuffled living arrangements, Amber seemed (at least for the time being, and to outward appearances) to develop into a relatively cheerful child who led the regular life of a suburban girl. Her best friend and fellow Sundling Junior High School class of 1996 graduate, Heather Lowing, recalls Amber fondly - 'I remember her being happy. She was just a very normal, junior high girl. I don't remember her missing school because she ran away, or talking about an awful home life.'

However, within six months all of that would change. As she entered her freshman year of high school, Amber sunk into a deep and crippling depression. Seeking some kind of temporary relief from her despair, she turned to drugs and alcohol. 'She didn't want to deal with it,' Robert Creek later said. She would act out by repeatedly running away from home for brief stints or by sneaking out of the house at night to meet older boys. Her cousin, Desiree Reeves, recalls 'She told me she was in the woods with a few boys. I remember asking her, "Why? Why do you sneak out?" I was scared for her. I was.'

Amber's family photo album tells a sad story. Within that six month period, Amber changes from a smiling, long-haired, makeup-less, All-American girl next door wearing bright clothing, to a blank-staring, dark-dyed and short-haired, made-up Lolita wearing black. It is common for those suffering from depression to seek to change their image in the belief that by transforming themselves on the outside they can fix what is troubling them on the inside. Robert would later say Amber had 'spiralled down' during this period and that 'She did not have the ability to keep relationships.'

By December of 1996, Amber's self-destructive behavior had worsened to the point where her psychiatrist recommended an intensive course of residential therapy. Robert Creek was unable to afford the hefty $50,000 price tag to follow up on the recommended form of therapy, instead attaining outpatient therapy for his daughter through a local hospital. His insurance did not cover this therapy for very long though, and when it ran out, he says 'She would come back home and the problems started again. Our psychiatrist wanted her in a locked-in facility. He said - and these are his exact words - "Someone is going to kill her if we do not do something." She was putting herself into more dangerous situations.'

Frustrated with the amount of red tape in the system, Robert pleaded with the DCFS to take Amber into their care but they refused. In a desperate move, he took her to the Palatine Police Department and told the officers present that Amber could no longer live in his house. This forced the DCFS' hand. Robert relinquished Amber into their temporary custody as a ward of the state. Subsequent unsuccessful attempts to place Amber in a foster home saw her entered into a group home situation at a North Chicago youth shelter, the Columbus-Maryville Center.

Amber continued her chronic runaway behavior during her stay at the center. By late 1996 she had ran away nine times, staying for only twenty-nine of the forty-four days that she was supposed to be living there. When she would run away, she would inevitably return to her father's home. On January 23, 1997, Amber ran away again. This time, she would never return home. Robert sensed that his troubled daughter had ran away for good this time - 'I knew when she was gone. She would have called home. She was never gone more than three days.' Amber did place phone calls to other relatives during this time, but she refused to reveal where she was staying. Attempting to make it on her own on the mean streets of Chicago, and without any money with which to purchase food to fill her belly, sadly Amber resorted to prostitution in desperation. On Saturday February 1, 1997, Amber's new wild lifestyle found her attending a weekend-long booze-soaked party at a Motel 6 with a group of older men in Rolling Meadows. At one point some police officers attended the party to perform a regulation check-up but they did not spot Amber, nor were they aware that she was currently a missing person whom they should have picked up if they had have seen her. Amber was witnessed leaving the party with a Caucasian male aged in his 30s. He was clean-shaven, of average height and medium to heavy build with brown hair and eyes. He was wearing a shirt and tie. They drove away in a large, gray, late model four-door luxury car, possibly a Lincoln. It had gray leather seats and a placard on the dashboard reading 'Mayor' against a white background. This was the last time that Amber was seen alive.

On February 9, 1997, a pair of men hunting in the Karcher Wildlife Area in the town of Burlington, Wisconsin made a gruesome discovery. Amber's frozen and battered corpse was lying in a marsh. It had been a brutal death and the killer seemed to have posed the body. It appeared to be a sexually motivated homicide. She had been bashed and raped, bitten savagely on the neck with great force and slashed about the face. She had been suffocated with a garbage bag which she still wore around her head. One arm was propped up against a tree as if to mimic a friendly wave and the word 'Hi' was written on her palm in black marker. Also affixed to her arm was a $5 price tag that had come from a *Golden Book* sold at a bookstore in Woodfield Mall in Schaumberg, Illinois.

The killer may have been signifying that Amber was cheap garbage. Some interpret the message as 'High-5.' Racine County Sheriff Chris Schmaling would later comment 'I'll tell you one thing: she did not deserve this. To be left here, just left like trash. It's sad and tragic. I have a 14-year-old daughter at home. I can't imagine if I lost her. Amber's parents looked all over Illinois. Her dad searched the streets. I don't think it would have crossed his mind that his daughter was lying dead in the cold in Wisconsin. I can't even fathom what that must be like. That's one reason why this case has never gone cold. It's so easy to forget about these cases after a couple decades, but I refuse to shelve these cases.'

Amber's body may have been posed as a sick joke intended to shock whoever eventually found her. She was naked from the waist down. The pants Amber had been wearing were discovered in a nearby parking lot with her panties stuffed into one of the pockets. Conspicuously absent were two possessions that Amber was never seen without - her distinctive forest-green winter jacket with a leather lapel and her dark green backpack on which she had drawn the 'Starter' logo in pencil. Within was poetry she wrote, cosmetics and photographs of her half-siblings. The murderer may have taken these items as trophies and to fuel later sexual homicide fantasies. Investigators gathered that Amber had been killed by one of her johns. At a 1999 FBI National Center for the Analysis of Violent Crime regional training conference, a member of the Amber Creek Homicide Task Force stated that 'because of Amber's high-risk lifestyle as a chronic runaway and prostitute who engaged in drug use, it was very possible that one of her clients had killed her.' Friends of Amber dispute the claims that she was a prostitute and drug addict. After the grisly find, investigators hid cameras in the area in an effort to capture the killer in case they returned to the scene of the crime, but no one did.

Amber was not identified immediately. The Columbus-Maryville Center failed to report her missing for a full five weeks after she disappeared from the shelter. When they did finally file the report they provided the wrong girl's photograph. Amber became a Jane Doe, and it was under this placeholder name that she was buried. The sad story of the unidentified, pretty, young murder victim that no one had claimed hit the headlines and touched the community. One hundred Wisconsinites turned out to Jane Doe's funeral so that the unfortunate girl might have someone to mourn her passing. A local man who had been moved by the story donated the casket and sheriff's deputies served as pallbearers.

Unaware that his daughter was dead by this stage, Robert Creek drove around Chicago and its suburbs searching for Amber for more than a year – 'It's a terrible thing to be driving around and see someone and have to turn back to see if it was her... It never was.'

Investigators had expended thousands of man-hours attempting to match fingerprints, DNA and dental records to their missing person files to no avail. It would take until June 26, 1998 for Amber's body to be positively identified through dental and DNA matches. *America's Most Wanted* had profiled the case that year. Robert Creek had viewed the episode and contacted police to inform them that he believed that Jane Doe was his daughter. When authorities finally realized who they had, more than a year after her death, Amber was reburied with a new, personal headstone at Holy Family Catholic Cemetery, Caledonia, Wisconsin. The stone reads: *Amber Creek, July 1982 – Feb. 1997. Earth has no sorrow that Heaven cannot heal, "You are so loved."*

Realizing that the Columbus-Maryville Center's initial inaction and mistakes had hindered the investigation, state laws regarding reporting of runaways were altered in direct response to Amber's case to prevent this from happening again. Illinois social workers initially denied that they had delayed reporting the disappearance. The Illinois DCFS insisted the disappearance was reported promptly on January

23, 1997. A Chicago police spokesperson said that there was no report filed that day.

Early investigations after Amber's identification focused on a pair of local men who often ran afoul of the Palatine and Rolling Meadows police departments, and who had also been in attendance at the Motel 6 party. However, DNA analysis eventually cleared these men of any wrongdoing. Fliers were distributed, a hotline was opened and fingerprint samples from the garbage bag were sent to the FBI and law enforcement agencies in 49 states. Detective John Hanrahan said 'Whoever killed Amber has kind of relaxed and settled in and no one came knocking. I can only imagine his stress level must be rising knowing that sooner or later we'll be knocking on his door.' For some time investigators ran out of leads to pursue and Amber's murder investigation stagnated.

In October of 2013 an Oklahoma forensics laboratory started to re-examine fingerprints lifted from various unsolved homicide cases. In February of 2014 the case was re-opened when Stacy Hirschman, an examiner at the Oklahoma laboratory, got a hit on a thumbprint found on the garbage bag that had covered Amber's face. It belonged to one James Paul Eaton, a 36-year-old Chicago Private Bank & Trust Company employee from Palatine. He had an ex-wife of 3 ½ years. The couple did not have any children. Eaton was nineteen years old at the time of Amber's death and his description closely resembled that of a man seen with Amber in February 1997. Eaton's fingerprints had not been matched at the time Amber's body was discovered as he was not in the system yet. He had not had any dealings with police until a 2000 arrest for possession of drug paraphernalia.

Hirschman contacted Agent Eric Szatkowski of the Wisconsin Department of Justice's Criminal Investigation Division to report the matched print. He was shocked when he heard the news - 'I literally almost fell off my chair in my office!' Investigators tracked Eaton down in Chicago and began several days of surveillance on him. On a March

22 stakeout they witnessed Eaton smoke several cigarettes outside the downtown Palatine Metra train station whilst he awaited his train which was running late, discarding the butts on the ground as he finished them. When Eaton left the scene the investigators recovered the cigarette butts. DNA from the cigarette butts was then matched to semen recovered through rectal swabbing at the crime scene. Police arrested Eaton in early April. Stacy Hirschman said 'I saw the print and just did my job and searched it, just wanting to ID that print. I'm just glad he's off the streets. Hopefully the family can have some peace.' Amber's aunt as well as family friends called Hirschman to personally thank her. A colleague had bet her a dinner that she would not get a hit on the almost two-decade-old fingerprints – 'He was quite stunned. He was silent for a bit. He definitely owed me dinner.' During interrogation, investigators endeavored to elicit an admission of guilt from Eaton. They showed him pictures of Amber while she was still alive. Eaton calmly denied ever having met her. They showed him crime scene pictures of Amber's body. He did not display a reaction.

Racine County Sheriff Christopher Schmaling told the media 'Today by far was the best moment for my investigative team as we informed Amber's dad that we caught her killer. It was an emotional exchange for everyone in the room. I couldn't be more proud of my investigative team today. Their hard work and commitment is unmatched. Today is a fantastic day to make a wonderful announcement to bring some closure to the Creek family. This is a day that we have been waiting more than seventeen years to arrive. We have solid, clear and overwhelming evidence that the suspect was responsible for Creek's death. Over the last seventeen years we have dedicated thousands of investigative hours to bring this tragic and senseless murder to its resolution. Today that day is here. Eaton had not previously been a suspect, nor was he even mentioned in our investigative reports. Our sense of accomplishment is tempered by the pain and loss we know Amber's family continues to confront every day.

Our thoughts and prayers remain with Amber's father, mother, other family and loved ones. We believe there are people out there who have knowledge of Mr Eaton and his involvement in the crime. We ask those people to search their hearts, do the right thing for Amber and her family, and come forward. While it is a great moment for the family to have closure, they are also asking for privacy to deal with their grief.' Palatine police Commander Dave Daigle echoed these sentiments – 'We have never arrested him. The only contact we've had is he received a speeding ticket and he was a victim of a burglary to his motor vehicle.'

Amber's aunt, Nowra Mowers said 'We are elated, absolutely, that someone has been caught in this crime. We've been waiting seventeen years. After seventeen years, my sister never gave up hope and my mother did not. She did not deserve to die in this way. Nobody deserves to die in this way. I want to know about him. Did he kill other people? Is she the only victim?'

Racine County Chief Deputy John Hanrahan, who was one of the top investigators in Amber's case from the beginning, gave a scathing indictment of the DCFS' handling of Amber's case at the time of her disappearance – 'Not only was the care and security they provided her extraordinarily inadequate, their failure to report Amber missing until well after she was found murdered is simply incredible. Amber and her family deserved much more.' Hanrahan had previously told the media in 1999 'Delays in identifying Amber's body have put us behind the 8-ball when it comes to tracking her killer. I believe this is a solvable case. I've got twenty years before I leave. This case will be worked on for at least the next twenty years.'

Many people, including Amber's uncle Anthony Mowers, believe that Eaton did not act alone in the murder. He speculates that Eaton may have had assistance in crossing interstate with Amber and that they may have lured Amber into a car under the pretence of offering her a lift to her grandmother's house (the grandmother lived in Wisconsin at the time). Police share Mowers' suspicion that Eaton did not act alone.

It is currently unknown if the human bite mark on Amber's neck came from Eaton, fuelling public speculation that Eaton had an accomplice or accomplices. Eaton's saliva, however, was located at the crime scene.

One of those present at a pre-trial hearing was Anthony Mowers, who stated 'I'm here for Amber. Just imagine how scared she must have been. I have no clue who this guy is. Nobody in the family does. This guy had to know this area. I don't know how the hell he got to that spot. He had to have somebody else along. Why would he drive there? How did he find this place? That's what I'm wondering, if it was some sort of partying. I wonder if he's got an ace up his sleeve. He's gotta have another perp involved. I don't understand - this guy's from Palatine. Maybe she thought he was taking her to her grandmother's house. There's no way she would have been in the car with him that long. At least not without putting up a fight. I'm still thinking he killed her in Illinois.'

Eaton shuffled into the hearing clad in orange Racine County Jail scrubs and sat quietly with his head down throughout the proceedings, while Mowers struggled to barely contain his rage, glaring at Eaton and clenching his jaw all the while. Racine County District Attorney Rich Chiapete pointed to Eaton and said 'This is an individual that has hid from the law for seventeen years. This case is chilling. It is a sad, savage, brutal attack. The bite mark was so significant it was a major and primary cause of her death here. We have an innocent, 14-year-old victim here. She was dumped like she was garbage.'

Amber's mother told the press 'Oh God, I knew I should have taken her. I didn't think they'd ever find this person. I'm so happy for that.' Her decision not to re-apply for custody of Amber at the time when she was placed in state care haunts her to this day. Eaton was held in the Racine County jail on $1 million bail. After the hearing Anthony Mowers exploded at a Racine County sheriff's investigator who walked up to him outside the courtroom and asked for his name. Mowers began yelling and ranting at the plain clothed investigator before storming out. But Mowers later hugged the man after realizing that he had investigating Amber's death and wanted to discuss the case. Mowers had mistaken the man for an Eaton supporter – 'He stared me down in the courtroom. I thought it was one of the Eaton family members. He shouldn't have come at me like that. I'm looking at a monster that killed my niece.'

Eaton was charged with murder one and concealing a body, which would have attracted a life sentence in prison. In October of 2014 Eaton pleaded not guilty to both charges at his arraignment. The trial proper was to begin in November 2015. Defense for the accused argued that the prosecution had not made available all of its evidence at discovery. The trial was then delayed until June 6, 2016 as the defense tried to find a man they contended had bitten Amber's neck so as to inspect his potential dental match as well as compare his DNA to that recovered at the crime scene. The judge threw out certain evidence supplied by the prosecution in relation to Eaton's interrogation when Eaton's attorney successfully argued that police had denied Eaton's requests to speak to a lawyer. In ignoring this request and continuing to interrogate Eaton, anything he might have said after that point was not permissible in court – 'Mr Eaton unequivocally and unambiguously invoked his right to counsel on April 5. At that point, all interrogation and questioning of Mr Eaton was to cease,' Racine County Circuit Court Judge Eugene Gasiorkiewicz said. The requests for counsel in question made by Eaton are as follows: 1 – 'I really think you guys need to get me a lawyer 'cause this is getting crazy;' 2 – 'I think you guys need to get me a lawyer 'cause this is crazy;' and 3 – 'I need to talk to a lawyer.'

It was only after Eaton's third request that detectives suspended the interrogation. Sheriff's Investigator Thomas Knaus testified that he ceased interrogating Eaton on April 5 after the third time he requested to speak to a lawyer. Knaus said that he had originally given Eaton a telephone book so that he could call a lawyer himself - 'I think he said he didn't have an attorney, so he didn't accept the phone book.' Upon cross-examination Knaus also admitted that he did not allow Eaton the opportunity to contact family members for the purposes of hiring a lawyer, nor did he call the Cook County Public Defender's Office to organize for a lawyer to meet with Eaton. Judge Gasiorkiewicz said that by investigators continuing to interrogate Eaton after his requests they had violated of his Fifth and Sixth Amendment rights, which pertain to not incriminating oneself and the right to a lawyer. Obviously it is not known what Eaton said during the time when the interrogation was in violation, but during the hearing Judge Gasiorkiewicz did say that 'He denied any ability to recognize Amber. Mr Eaton did not physically react when shown those photos. They were unsuccessful in obtaining a confession.'

Eaton pleaded no contest to a lesser charge of first-degree reckless homicide on October 25, 2016. A plea of no contest occurs when a defendant neither admits nor denies the charges. It is rather an acknowledgement that the defendant concedes that the prosecution would likely be successful in gaining a conviction against them based on the evidence, were the case to go to trial. Whilst not technically a guilty plea, it has the same instant effect. At the time of writing Eaton has yet to be sentenced, but he is facing up to 40 years in prison once this takes place. He is currently imprisoned in Racine, Wisconsin. Whilst most people consider that Eaton murdered Amber Creek, he is not without his supporters. Some people posit that Eaton met Amber at the Motel 6 party, had consensual sex with her that night, gave her the plastic bag for whatever reason, and was killed by her pimp for failing to charge Eaton. A second man, whose name has not yet been released, is also currently under investigation for alleged connection to the crime.

WHEN THE GIRL NEXT DOOR KILLS: THE TRUE STORY OF TYLAR WITT

ERICA FOSTER

"At round one in the morning, the girl snuck the boy into her house. He stabbed her in her sleep, killing her and freeing themselves." This was an excerpt from fourteen year old Tylar Witt's story entitled, "The Killer and his Raven." A story she wrote about her own mother's brutal murder.

Tylar Witt lived in an upscale neighborhood in El Dorado Hills, California with her forty seven year old single mother, Joanne Witt. Joanne worked for the county as an assistant engineer for the Department of Transportation and they lived in an elegant house in a nice gated community. Tylar was a fourteen year old girl who was entering her freshman year at Oak Ridge High School. She was described as a sweet girl when she was growing up. Her mother paid for riding lessons and they liked to stay at home and watch movies and cook, but as Tylar grew up, the behavioral problems began and the fights between the mother and daughter turned into physical altercations. Tylar was turning into a different person, she was becoming a monster.

It all started out as what looked like typical teenage rebellion. Tylar embraced the emo and gothic lifestyle by wearing dark and baggy clothes, she had a love of anime and Japanese cartoons, along with everything violent and connected with death. Tylar met her 'Romeo', nineteen year old Steven Colver, at a coffee shop in the popular shopping center of Town Center Shops, where they both frequented. As Tylar was entering her first year of high school, Steven was beginning his first year of college. He was employed as a Shift Lead at Rubio's Mexican Grill. The duo quickly became inseparable. Tylar looked at the older boy as a god and worshiped everything about him. There wasn't anything she wouldn't do for him. The two were in love.

It was in April of 2009, a few weeks after the two had met, that Tylar approached her mother. She convinced her mother that Steven was gay, so that he would be allowed to rent the extra room in their family home. After much resistance from family and friends, Joanne defended the decision by saying that Steven would be helping her make the mortgage payment, as well as help Tylar with her homework. She was described as very strong-willed by her friends and family and didn't let their opinion of others affect her decision to let Steven move in. Joanne didn't suspect a relationship between Steven and her daughter until one day in May, about a month after Steven had moved in. She entered Steven's room and found Steven and Tylar about to engage in a sexual relationship, or had just finished. She found Tylar naked and hiding in Steven's closet, trying to cover herself up. Joanne was understandably upset and demanded that Steven immediately move out. She called two of her male coworkers to come over and assist her. Joanne informed them that she was kicking Steven out of her house and she didn't want to be alone when she did it in case anything were to happen. The male coworkers helped place all of Steven's belongings on the sidewalk and even threatened Steven before he left.

Vinnie Capatano, one of Joanne's coworkers helping her that day, threatened Steven, "If you make contact with Tylar again, either by phone or in person- I am going to hurt you. And I am going to hurt you East Coast style, not West Coast style." It was an act intended to promote intimidation and scare tactics. Steven looked unshaken, which annoyed Capatano even further. His words didn't seem to bother Steven at all.

Joanne was convinced that Steven had committed a crime by sleeping with her underage daughter and made that clear to Steven before he left. She threatened to go to the police and file statutory rape charges if Steven ever came into contact with her daughter again. He didn't take Joanne's words seriously, or the threats of her coworkers. Steven was later found at least twenty more times after this encounter, sneaking into Joanne's house. All Joanne wanted to do was get her daughter away from this older boy that seemed to influence her bad behavior and irrational decisions. Joanne acted as any other mother in this situation would.

Despite the threats, Steven and Tylar continued their love affair and sexual relationship during the day while Joanne was at work and late at night while Joanne was sleeping. Joanne had expressed concern to a few of her coworkers about her daughter's behavior and the boy that seemed able to control and influence her so greatly. It wasn't long until Joanne found out what was going on behind her back and continued to make good on her promise of going to the police. Steven and Tylar vowed to find a way to stay together, no matter the cost. This is the moment the plotting began between the modern day Romeo and Juliet. This was about a month before Joanne Witt was found dead in her home and arrest warrants were issued for her daughter and her daughter's boyfriend.

Joanne Witt located her daughter's diary and handed it over to the police that were handling the statutory rape complaint. The diary clearly outlined the sexual relationship between Tylar Witt and Steven Colver. It explicitly described numerous sexual positions and encounters that the two had shared. There was no mistaking that there was definitely a sexual relationship happening between Steven and Tylar. The detective called to interview Steven about the allegations and Steven claimed that he was worried about Tylar, but their relationship was platonic. He said he considered Tylar as more of a sister figure, than anything else, and he denied any sexual relationship between the two of them. He also admitted that he was scared of this whole situation and he knew she was only fourteen years old. The relationship between Tylar and her mother was volatile and destructive, to say the least, even before she turned in the diary.

Joanne was a loving and attentive single mother that made her daughter, Tylar, the center of her world. However, an incident that took place when Tylar was five years old, prompted an investigation that removed her only daughter from her home. Tylar was placed into foster care for a brief time before Joanne's parents, Norb and Judi Witt could take her in. Tylar lived with them for 6 months while Joanne attended anger management and parenting classes. The incident occurred when Tylar was just five years old after

Joanne had picked her up from daycare. The young girl was screaming in the backseat which was causing Joanne to lose patience very quickly. Joanne reached back and slapped Tylar. The daycare saw the hand shaped mark on Tylar and immediately reported the abuse to CPS, Child Protective Services.

After Tylar was finally able to go back home to her mother, Joanne was afraid to discipline her like she had before. This gave Tylar the opportunity to do whatever she wanted, knowing she could get away with it. Tylar would threaten to call CPS and report her mother again if she didn't get what she wanted. This created many behavioral problems for Tylar and this manifested itself in the violent relationship between the mother and the daughter. Tylar also reported that her mother was a heavy drinker and she would hit and punch Tylar when she was mad. These allegations were never proven. If the violence and abuse had been as severe as Tylar had made it sound, there would have been noticeable marks and bruises on Tylar. They never found any evidence of the abuse she claimed was taking place at the home. There was constant fighting and arguing. Joanne didn't feel comfortable enough start disciplining her daughter again until the few months before that led up to her murder.

The day that Joanne admitted to taking her daughter's diary into the police, was the same night that Joanne and Tylar got into a horrendous fight at home. Tylar felt betrayed by her mother's actions and began throwing objects at her and fighting with her. Tylar called 911 pretending to be Joanne in an attempt to be taken out of the home. She would have rather been in the Juvenile Detention Center than at home with her mother that night. Joanne got onto the phone with dispatch and when they asked her if she was okay, she responded no. Deputies were on their way to the residence. When the police arrived they saw a cut on Joanne's chin and several bruises. Tylar was taken in that night but was released only hours later, after Joanne refused to press charges against her daughter. Joanne was never required to go to the hospital due to her injuries.

Norbert Witt, Tylar's grandfather, claimed that Steven was a bad influence on his granddaughter, and said that he corrupted her by exposing her to sex and heavy narcotics. Steven was known to engage in illegal narcotics such as marijuana, ecstasy, and cocaine.

Norb and Judi Witt owned a luxury RV and had spent the previous two months traveling around the country. They arrived home only days before they received the call that would turn their world upside down. It was Monday when they received a call from Joanne's boss inquiring if they had any idea as to the whereabouts of their daughter. Joanne had an impeccable work history and never missed work without first calling to let them know. So, when Joanne didn't show up or call that Friday, her coworkers began to worry. They stopped by her home that night and knocked on the door, but there was no answer. Nobody seemed to be home. After Joanne didn't show up to work the following Monday either, they knew something was terribly wrong and called the police to report Joanne as missing. After speaking to Joanne's parents and informing them that they had already contacted the police, they raced over to their daughter's house, which was only a few miles away, so they could check themselves. It is there that they met the police. Norb Witt let them into the house to search. The police informed Joanne's parents that she was found upstairs in her room, and she was deceased. There was no sign of a break in or forced entry, there was nothing missing in the home. But where was Tylar? Better yet, where were Tylar and her older boyfriend?

It didn't take the police long to realize that Tylar and Steven had something to do with the cruel and heinous crime in the Witt house. It was only weeks earlier that Joanne had reported Steven to the police and turned in Tylar's diary. She made her feelings about her mother known in the words scrawled throughout the pages. Tylar even plastered her contempt for her mother across her social media sites. She wasn't shy when it came to sharing her feelings and opinion of her mother.

Tylar and Steven went on like normal the days following the murder. They were living the life they wanted now that Tylar's mother wasn't there to get in the middle of it and stop it. They were seen holding hands and kissing, and had seen some of their friends. It was after a night of smoking marijuana and doing lines of cocaine at Steven's father's house that Steven confessed to murdering Joanne and even showed his friend the bloody knife that he was hiding in the car. This friend was Matthew Wildman. Wildman later testified against Steven and told the court that Steven did indeed show him the knife that was used, and he described how the murder happened, and how Steven stood there when he was finished and watched Joanne die. Steven's father came home unexpectedly so they all left the house, with the murder weapon. The murder weapon was never retrieved after their arrest.

The couple had fled to San Francisco, they no longer cared about the consequences because their plan all along was to commit suicide. If they weren't there, they wouldn't have to face the murder charges. According to their logic, that was the only way that they would be able to stay together, without interference, as well as keep Steven out of jail because of the statutory rape charges. They thought the charges would carry a heavy prison sentence and they didn't want to risk separation due to the diary that Joanne had turned into the police earlier.

While in San Francisco, they rented a hotel room and consumed a bazaar mix of fruit loops, cake and rat poison and each had written out suicide notes. The combination of food mixed with the rat poison didn't work, however, and they were arrested shortly after, before they had a second chance to commit suicide. Alongside the food that was found in the hotel room, police also found marijuana, condoms, Steven's work apron and nametag, and the movie 'Donnie Darko' on DVD. They were found changing clothes behind a dumpster at a shopping mall in the area and were arrested by local police and taken in for questioning regarding Joanne Witt's murder.

Once in custody, Tylar refused to admit that she knew her mother was dead and admitted no fault. She asked for a lawyer and for the detectives to go away. The fateful night her mother was brutally murdered was June 11, 2009. Well into the night, after Joanne had finally fallen asleep, Tylar let Steven into the house. He had acquired a chef's knife from his restaurant job at Rubio's. Tylar had grabbed a knife out of the kitchen in her house, and the two proceeded to go upstairs to the bedroom where Joanne Witt was fast asleep. They had each planned to use the knives they had to kill Joanne....together. Tylar claimed that she could not go into the room with Steven. She fell to her knees and covered her ears, while humming to drown out the sound of her mother being stabbed to death. Steven had taken several practice slashes in the air as a warm up before going into Joanne's room and Tylar said this is what prompted her to stay outside of the room. She chose not to go in with Steven. Joanne was stabbed around twenty times. The fatal wound was a gaping slash in her neck. She struggled with her killer and had put her hands up in defense but the wounds were too severe. A bloody knife outline was left on the bed and a book entitled, "How to Parent your Out-Of-Control Teenager, was ironically nestled in the nightstand next to her bed. Tylar and Steven covered Joanne's body with a blanket, turned the air conditioner down in an attempt to preserve the body, and locked up the house and left. They decided to jump the fence instead of having to put the code in to get out. They didn't want anyone to place them there at the time of the murder.

In a suicide letter that Steven had written to his friends, as a kind of apology for what he had done, he said, "Our souls are tainted...We shall be awaiting our fate in the afterworld."

After the news of Joanne's murder got around, a neighbor spoke up about allegedly speaking to Tylar in the park a few months prior. The neighbor had been walking her daughter to the park and claimed she saw a young girl that looked alone, sad, and even angry. The girl was sitting on the swing set with her face toward the ground. She confronted her and asked what was wrong. She said the girl described a bad home life with her mother, and mentioned that her mother liked to drink and would get violent and hurt her, and they would get into a lot of fights. She said the girl seemed really cold and lost in her replies. When asked what Tylar was going to do to stop it the next time it happened she simply replied, "There isn't going to be a next time. Next time it is going to be either her or me." This statement stuck with the neighbor for a long time after. When she realized that the crime scene was a daughter that killed her mother, she finally spoke to police about the conversation in the park. The neighbor was seen on news footage talking to one of the police on the scene, but requested that her name be left out of the media.

Dan Weiner, Steven's attorney, claimed that it was not Steven that committed the murder, it was Tylar. When describing her relationship with Steven, Tylar said, "I trusted him more than I trusted anyone. And I love him more than anybody or anything. If he told me to jump off a bridge and I asked him why and he said just trust me, I would have done it." This shows just how much influence Steven had over Tylar. When neighbors of Steven's were asked to describe him they had only nice things to say.

"He's always been a nice kid as far as I am concerned. If this is true, it is out of character." –Paul Matloff. He also described Steven as a stand-up kid that never played his music too loudly and was always eager to help his neighbors.

Joan Colver, Steven's mother was quoted by reporters as saying, "He would care about others before himself. Steven is the kind of guy who would drive off a cliff or jump in front of a bullet or run into a burning building....for a friend."

When asked why Weiner felt that Steven was being targeted for performing the actual murder instead of Tylar, he didn't really know why. He backed up his defense and Steven's statement of Tylar being the one to murder Joanne Witt, given her past history compared to Steven's.

"He has never hurt anybody, or tried to hurt anybody or threatened to hurt anybody. As contrasted with Tylar who has a very specific history with her mother, and has literally threatened to kill her, to stab her...the very method by which she was ultimately killed!"

Steven had changed his story and said that Joanne was already dead by the time he arrived at the Witt house that night.

"I think realizing the gravity of the situation after being in jail for a while, it took a while before he was willing to confirm, yeah, that she had done it and how she had done it."

Steven said that Tylar stabbed her own mother to death and then called him over to the house after it was done. That is when he claims to have seen the bloody knife. He said that there was blood dripping everywhere, including some spots on Tylar's pants, but there was no evidence of blood droplets being found anywhere else in the house. It was all confined to Joanne's bedroom where she was murdered. The defense claimed that the police failed to look for blood anywhere else except for the primary focus of the house, which was the bedroom. Therefore, there was no evidence available to back up Steven's story. This new story also came about after Steven had already described to his friends how he stabbed his girlfriend's mother to death in her sleep with a butcher knife. Weiner said that Steven was not homicidal, rather suicidal. They claimed that the plan was for Steven to pick up Tylar and they would run off to San Francisco for a few days and then commit suicide together. There was no talk of murdering Joanne. The defense also mentioned that Steven had a clean record, while Tylar's was filled with a history of violence and running away. Despite the new story, Steven's confession to his friend was more than the prosecution needed. He was convicted based on his own words, just as his mother had predicted earlier.

In prosecutor Lisette Suder's words in her opening statement at trial, she described the couple's actions as "a

19 year old man and a 14 year old girl and their love affair that led to the violent almost to the point of sadistic murder of her mother." Tylar was portrayed as an extremely manipulative and brilliant girl. After lying to the detectives when she was first taken into custody and questioned, she finally decided to tell the truth and later passed a polygraph test proving it. She admitted to conspiring with Steven to kill her mother, but also said that it was Steven that committed the actual murder, while she lay in a fetal position outside of the bedroom. All of the evidence found on the scene corroborated Tylar's account of the events from that night. Tylar, in exchange for her testimony against Steven, received a reduced sentence of fifteen years to life for second degree murder. She would be eligible for parole at the age of twenty nine, instead of thirty nine. They were both sentenced at the El Dorado County Superior Court in Placerville.

Joanne Witt's brother, Michael, shared his feelings before sentencing. He was the one that had been responsible for cleaning up his sister's home after the murder. He said he would never be able to get the images of the crime scene photos out of his head.

"I hope and desire that Mr. Colver experiences the worst possible experiences our wonderful prison system can bestow upon him." The judge had tried several times to stop Matthew's rant.

The trial began with Steven still trying to protect Tylar. He didn't want people to accuse his love, Tylar, of being the mother killer. In the beginning stages of his questioning he would ask investigators if they had spoken with Tylar and he inquired about her well-being. He was sympathetic to her situation and just wanted to help her. He thought they were in it together and their love would keep them connected. It ended with the scorned lovers passing the blame to each other. Steven's defense referred to him as an easily manipulated love-struck teen.

Steven's trial lasted for four weeks but the verdict only took four hours to come back. With Tylar's account of the events, the confession Steven made to his friends, and the DNA found underneath Joanne's fingernails that linked the homicide to a male attacker, it all led Steven to a verdict of guilty, for first degree murder. He was sentenced to life in prison without the possibility of parole.

After sentencing, however, Tylar had an interview in which she admitted, "I still have a really hard time being honest. I panic when I get in trouble and the first thing I want to do is lie to get out of it." This statement could potentially be enough to seek an appeal for Steven Colver at a later date. It showed just how dishonest Tylar could be. So if she were able to say this now, what if everything she said in the trial was a lie, despite the polygraph test.

Tylar's psychologist referred to her as a sociopath. Tylar, in trial, said she had three different personalities that were living inside of her. She had her own personality, an angel named Alex, and a demon she referred to as Toby. She claimed her violent actions that led up to this point were because of the demon. Toby would come in times of intense stress. Tylar also described blackouts that she would experience when she was enraged and tried to use the compassion of her dead mother to sway the jury in her favor.

"My mom was not a vicious person and she didn't hold grudges. Even if something horrible like this would have happened, she would have asked for a just punishment. She wouldn't want to see someone suffer for the rest of their lives for a mistake they made when they were being ignorant and stupid."

The following is a letter that Tylar allegedly wrote to her mother before she was murdered. It was Tylar's plan to run away and commit suicide. It was a good bye letter addressed to Joanne.

"As much as you don't think I love you, I do. Not just because I am your daughter but because you are my best friend. Nothing I have ever said to you in anger was ever true. I would never kill you or hate you....but I can't stand to see you so unhappy, but I am growing up and seeing as you don't love me....the person I have become, I see it only fit I do one last thing to make you happy. You want me gone? I am gone."

In Tylar's testimony she admitted the act of violence toward her mother was not a spontaneous decision. It was a decision Steven and Tylar had made after thoroughly discussing their options.

"I was in shock and then I went into a full blown panic attack, hyperventilating, screaming, and shaking." This was in response to Tylar finding out that her mother had turned her diary over to the police in an attempt to build a case against Steven. They came to their own realization that the only way to save Steven from jail was to murder her mother. There was no way they wouldn't file the charges after all the proof was in the diary. They didn't see another way out.

Steven and Tylar concocted this murder plan, afraid that Steven would be sent to prison for a long time because of the statutory rape charges Joanne had filed against him. They didn't want to risk being separated from each other. They saw the murder and subsequent double suicide as a way of staying together. Just like Romeo and Juliet. What they didn't know was that the statutory rape charges only carried a year worth of prison time, if there was any time at all; it was considered a misdemeanor. Instead of a small charge, with little or no prison time, they exchanged a lifetime of freedom for a lifetime of being locked away due to their irrational nature and horrid actions that were compelled by fear. Neither Tylar, nor Steven were able to determine exactly which one of them came up with the idea of killing Joanne. Tylar had been labeled a liar from the very beginning but all of the evidence they had matched with what Tylar had been saying about that night. Everything fit into place and that's why they believed she was finally telling the truth about Steven.

During Tylar's sentencing the judge addressed her directly, "This was a brutal murder. The court has seen no emotion or even remorse for the loss of your mother...I'm sorry for you Miss Witt, because the person who loved you most and without reservation is gone."

Judi Witt had waited a long time before she would go and visit her granddaughter. When she finally set eyes on Tylar she asked how she could have done such a horrible thing. A look of shock plastered across Tylar's face and she responded, "Do you really think I would have been able to do something like this?" When asked if Judi actually believed her, she responded yes.

Not only did they lose their daughter, Judi and Norb Witt also lost their granddaughter. Judi was able to forgive a little easier than Norb. Norb has since written his granddaughter off for killing his daughter. Her actions were inexcusable. She is not the same little girl that they remembered. They said that the Tylar they knew, wasn't the Tylar that killed Joanne. They choose to remember the little girl that they first visited in the hospital after her birth. Tylar was their third grandchild. They recalled the hospital visit after her birth very fondly. They walked in there with a camera and took many pictures, in awe of their own daughter and their new granddaughter. They choose to remember Tylar as the little girl they had watched grow up, not the monster she had become after killing her own mother, not the girl that constantly defied her own mother and threatened her. Not the girl that wrote in her diary about her dream of finding out her mother had died in a car accident. Tylar had lost her way a long time ago. They choose to only remember the good, but revealed that their family was never going to be the same either. Judi and Norb had come to terms with this.

Norb finally decided to go and see Tylar, after the trial. He had refused to go and see her up until this point. When Norb entered the room, Tylar called him Poppa and embraced him. She began sobbing. Norb held onto her tightly and said, after speaking with her, he could see some kind of remorse for what she had done but he still wasn't in the position of being able to forgive her. "It is hard to forgive someone that helped kill your daughter." Norb and Judi do not visit Tylar in prison, but they do say they write to her very often.

In later interviews Tylar finally began showing small signs of remorse for her mother's brutal ending. At one time Tylar had even considered her mom to be her hero and looked at her as not only a mother figure, but also as a father figure, since she never had a real father. Tylar's personalities were all over the place. She would love her mother one day but threaten to kill her the next.

Steven's mother still holds onto the hope of her son's innocence and the possibility of an appeal. She refuses to believe that the boy she knew would be capable of doing something so unforgivable and so violent to someone else.

The tragic death of Joanne Witt and the story of her daughter and her daughter's boyfriend being the murderers shook the community. A violent history with Joanne and her defiance of any kind of authority figures led Tylar into the arms of someone she felt could protect her. The two scorned lovers had a premeditated and thought out plan to kill the object of their resistance. According to their teenage logic, getting rid of Joanne and committing suicide was the only way they could ever be together. Even the most thought out plans tend to backfire, however, and they were very much alive while Joanne was gone. They traded a life of freedom with some restrictions, for a life spent behind bars. They miscalculated the situation and now live to regret it, day after day, year after year.

THE MISSING BEAUTY QUEEN: THE DISAPPEARANCE OF TARA GRINSTEAD

AMANDA DARLING

"I'm an 11th-grade history teacher at Irwin County High school. I also have a cheerleading squad of Junior Varsity cheerleaders. I just completed my first year of teaching, and I love every bit of it." - Tara Grinstead in a 1999 interview.

Tara Grinstead was a beauty pageant winner and high school teacher who strangely disappeared on October 22nd, 2005.

The mystery of her disappearance is as baffling now as it was over ten years ago. Tara was a beautiful woman in a small town and drew the attention of many men. But as investigators peeled back the onion on her life, they discovered that she had a complex personal life, one with many lovers and layers of relationship any one of whom may have sought to do her harm out of jealousy.

Investigators have pieced together the timeline of her activities prior to her disappearance. But the missing piece lies sometime during the night of October 22nd, 2005, when someone abducted Tara Grinstead and she would never be seen again.

What happened to Tara Grinstead?

EARLY LIFE

Tara was born on November 14th, 1974 to Faye and Billy Grinstead. She grew up in Hawkinsville, Georgia and was a popular cheerleader in high school as well as a diligent student. Her parents would divorce and her father would remarry a woman named Connie to whom Tara grew close to as well.

Tara loved animals, singing and going to church as a kid.

One cannot look upon pictures and video of Tara and not remark that she had a striking beauty. Graced with a voluptuous figure and long black hair, she had the ability to light up any room she walked into. She would eventually compete in beauty pageants, falling in love with the preparation, competition, and glamor of the activity.

"She had been into so many (pageants) that I had lost count," Connie Grinstead said.

Tara meticulously prepared for the pageants, remaining physically fit, taking speech lessons and learning how to sing. She would also graduate from Middle Georgia College and become a teacher at Irwin County High School in Ocilla. She would teach history to 11th graders but not give up on her pageant hopes.

In 1999, she would achieve the first step in her dream to enter the Miss USA contest, when she would win the local title of Miss Tifton.

This victory would allow her to compete in the Miss Georgia pageant. She would also receive scholarship winnings that she would use to help pay for her continuing college education.

"It was, for her, more than a dream come true," Tara's best friend Maria Hulett said. "It was the chance for her to be really proud of herself."

Footage of Tara during the Georgia pageant showed her to be an exuberant woman with a zest for life. She loved to exercise, drink Diet Coke with grenadine, collect Barbies and listening to 80s music like Bon Jovi. She had an infectious smile and played to the camera as she showed off her yellow business suit that she would wear for the pageant interview.

"Why did you pick yellow?" the reporter asked.

"Because it shows that I'm a happy person," Tara said.

With her pageant days behind her, Tara would earn a master's degree in education from Valdosta State University.

"She wanted to be a principal," her friend Oshja Anderson said. "She was well on her way."

Always seeking to improve herself, Tara would teach classes during the day and go to graduate school at night. She also held down a part-time job selling cosmetics at the local department store. By 2005, she had applied for a doctoral program in history and would occasionally fill in as the assistant principal.

"On the surface," forensic psychiatrist Orange said. "Tara's life looked to be a stellar one. She had a bright future in academia and during her pageant days, she learned to put forward the best appearance. But what lurked underneath in her personal life is the mystery."

MARCUS HARPER

At the heart of Tara's disappearance is figuring out the type of relationships she had with the numerous men in her life. She worked as a teacher, went to night school and worked the cosmetics counter at a department store. Outgoing and bubbly, she didn't have the personality type to reject anyone out of hand. She attracted men and had many suitors.

She did have a longtime boyfriend in Marcus Harper.

Harper was an Ocilla police officer who would later become an Army Ranger. Both of Tara's parents liked him as they both expressed the fact that he always remained respectful of them. They have consistently maintained that they never witnessed Harper treating Tara with disrespect.

Tara, however, had expressed to her sister that she was afraid of Marcus.

"She said she was afraid of him," Tara's sister Anita said. "What he had gone through with the Ranger training. He was capable of anything."

"Marcus was a strong Alpha-male type," Orange said. "A cop and an Army Ranger. Tara was rumored to have dated another cop as well but she didn't appear to have a type. From what we can gather, she dated a slew of men from older to younger, and from different walks of life."

About a year prior to her disappearance, Tara had broken up with Marcus. She had given him an ultimatum and wanted to be married. He did not want marriage but wanted to remain committed. The relationship would turn sour at that point.

Tara would begin to date other people. She was in a car with a romantic suitor named Rhett Roberts who was the son of her landlord.

Marcus spotted the couple and would go ballistic, shouting obscenities at Tara.

Despite this angry confrontation, Tara would maintain ties with Marcus. In late July or early August of 2005 they would go to St. Augustine on a beach trip. After their date, Tara would confide to a friend that she was concerned about Marcus's temper.

Marcus would then be deployed back to Iraq a few weeks later. Tara would write the Army Ranger a letter in which she effectively ended their relationship.

According to Marcus, however, their relationship didn't come to a close until October of 2005. He had returned from the Middle East and called Tara to tell her that their relationship was over. Tara was at work and became so distraught that had to pull over to the side of the road. She called a friend who came and took her home. The next day, Tara would call off sick from her teaching job in order to "take a mental health day."

There was a rumor that a cop from a neighboring town, Heath Dykes, came to visit Tara at her school shortly afterward.

"These behaviors certainly show some mental fragilities on the parts of both Tara and Marcus," Orange said. "From what we can gather, it looked like an off-and-on style relationship with a few other romantic partners thrown in for good measure. It is unclear as to who was chasing who at various points of their relationship. If we are to believe Marcus, then she was chasing him. If we are to believe Tara's sister, then she was afraid of him. Why would you chase a man that you were afraid of? Something is not right here."

A few days later, Tara and Marcus would have another "heated argument" which she would tell one of her friends at her night class as well as another friend the next day while she had lunch.

According to Marcus, the argument centered around him breaking up with her. But Tara's sister Anita Gattis had a different story.

"They had a very bad argument," Anita said. "Several days before she went missing, concerning an 18-year-old that he was dating. My sister did not think that (the 18-year-old's) parents would approve of a 30-year-old dating an-18-year-old. I'm told that she threatened to tell the parents and they had a very heated argument over this."

Marcus said the argument was about something else entirely. He stated that she begged him not to end their relationship.

"She wanted me back and all," Marcus said. "And I said, 'I've started shopping outside of Ocilla, I think you need to do the same. Everybody in this town is connected to us one way or another."

"She approached me crying," Harper said as he repeated the same story on Greta Van Susteren's TV show. "She was very irrational, and she told me that if she found out I was dating someone, she would commit suicide."

But Tara's friend Osjha disputes the fact that Tara would do or say something like that.

"She's never said anything remotely similar to me ever any time."

Law enforcement authorities don't believe Tara committed suicide as she would have to go to extreme lengths to hide her own body and would have no motive to do so.

"There are a couple of contradictory things at play here," Orange said. "Tara was rumored to have dated some of her students so it would be hypocritical of her to criticize Marcus for dating someone in their teens. And it also doesn't make sense for her to come to Marcus' home begging to get back together. She had her share of suitors, some coming from out of town. She was a beautiful woman and she had options."

To her family's dismay, both the authorities and press would place Tara's life under a microscope. They had discovered that she had "several romantic relationships that occurred in relative proximity to one another."

"There was more rumors and innuendo," Orange said. "There were rumors that she was dating Rhett Roberts, her landlord's son. Rumors that she was dating one of her teenage students. Rumors that she was dating Heath Dyke, a police officer from another county. Even her own brother-in-law, Larry Gattis, was rumored to have an affair with Tara."

Both Larry and Tara's sisters are physicians. Larry specializes in geriatric medicine with only 3.3 out of 5-star reviews on Healthgrades. He was interrogated by investigators and expressed his outrage at the questions they were asking. One question was that if he had an affair with Tara and his response was judged by the polygraph as "deceptive."

ALL THAT AND A STALKER TOO...

Tara would have a stalker in a former student named Anthony Vickers. Friends recalled that Tara had taken special care to tutor Vickers but she later realized that the young man was "unstable."

"He was just kind of a troubled kid and that would be her nature," Osjha said.

Vickers was obsessed with his beauty queen teacher and claimed to have had a romantic relationship with her.

"She talked about the fact that he would call and he would rely on her and she knew it was getting too much for her," a friend named Maria said. "I just kept telling her, 'You know Tara, something's wrong."

Vickers was two years out of high school when he came to Tara's house and demanded to be let in. He pounded on the door until she called the police. Vickers resisted arrest but charges were later dropped and no restraining orders were ever filed.

The Vickers incident wasn't the only occasion that the former beauty pageant winner was being stalked. There was an incident where someone would call her home and make threats. The call was traced and it was determined to be a student in her homeroom who was promptly removed from the class.

THE NIGHT OF...

Before the night of her disappearance, Tara had enjoyed the company of her friend Dana and some teenage girls as they readied for the "Miss Georgia Sweet Potato" pageant. Her friend remembered

Tara as being in a great mood, helping out the girls with their hair and makeup. She would attend the pageant where she served as a backstage coach. Later that evening, she went to the house of a neighbor before going to a barbecue a few blocks from her home . Police believe that she had remained at the barbecue until 11 pm when she left to go home. They would find the clothes she wore at the cookout on her bedroom floor which indicated to police that she had, in fact, returned home.

From that point on, police "have no idea" what happened to Tara.

On October 24th, 2005, Tara did not show up to teach her class. Her colleagues called the police who showed up at her residence to do a welfare check. They would find her white Mitsubishi parked in the garage, unlocked. Upon entering her home, police found a business card lodged in her door.

There appeared to be no sign of forced entry. Searching through the house, police found her cell phone plugged into her charger. Her purse and keys could not be found.

Strangely, the clothes she wore the night before were piled on the bedroom floor.

Investigators found it odd that the car door was unlocked and that the car seat was pushed back. Tara was petite at only five-foot-three and would have kept the seat much closer to the steering wheel. They found an envelope of cash (one hundred dollars) on her dashboard while both her dog and cat were inside. Tara's sister said that she was an animal lover who would never just abandon her pets.

Something was wrong...

The police immediately called the Georgia Bureau of Investigation as the lacked the resources to pursue this kind of crime.

Taking over the case, the GBI believed that Tara may have left with someone that she knew, given the lack of a forced entry and the fact that only her purse and keys were missing. Neighbors did not report hearing any screaming at night.

Her disappearance shocked the small and close-knit community. To a person, Tara was described as someone who had a great personality, loved by faculty and students alike. Nothing in her professional life would suggest that she had any enemies.

Volunteers from the community immediately went to work. Irwin County students, teachers, and other townsfolk searched the area and put out flyers.

"Missing. Tara Grinstead. $20,000 Reward."

ROUNDING UP THE SUSPECTS

Longtime boyfriend Marcus Harper was one of the first to be questioned. He came with a ready-made alibi for the night of Tara's disappearance.

Marcus was seen at a bar with friends then went on a 'ride-along' with a former partner on the local police force. His whereabouts was "essentially substantiated" according to authorities.

Former student/stalker Anthony Vickers was questioned but later ruled out as a suspect. Like the others, however, he could not account for the entire thirty-four hour period when Tara was last seen and reported missing.

"Vickers is probably the only one I would rule out," Orange said. "This disappearance was too clean. Vickers was a disturbed twenty-year-old man with a crush. He would not have the emotional wherewithal or the knowledge to pull off a crime with no clues. But someone with law enforcement or medical training could."

But who left the business card behind at her door?

The card was left by Heath Dykes, a married Perry police officer with two children. He was from the next town over and had known Tara since high school.

Neighbors would tell investigators that he visited Tara's house often. It is unclear what their relationship was (outside of the obvious innuendo and rumors).

Still, he had left close to two dozen messages on Tara's answering message on the weekend she went missing.

There is small-town gossip that the two were having an affair. Local witnesses have confirmed that they saw his wife throw his clothes out on the front lawn. The content of the messages he left have not been made public but the rumors were that he was telling her "he was sorry" and that he "loved her."

What is clear is that he did call Tara's mother from the front yard and ask if she knew where Tara was and if she was alright.

Heath Dykes was the last known person at Tara's home that night as he arrived a little after midnight.

"There are simply too many secrets here," Orange said. "Something was clearly going on in Heath's mind in order for him to call Tara that many times over the course of one evening. One rumor is that they were having an affair and that she was going to tell his wife. So he was calling her in a desperate attempt to stop her from doing that. Another possibility was that she was calling him for help and he was returning her calls. His involvement led to a lot of outlandish speculation, one of which was that Heath knew that a hit man was coming for Tara and that he was calling to make sure that she was okay."

"I think the fact that she was beautiful and other people paid attention to her would obviously make some people jealous," Tara's friend Maria said. "I think she was afraid of the possibility of someone hurting her from being angry at her, having reactions to her dating people."

Numerous men were rounded up and questioned, there was Jim Perry who dated Tara years earlier, Rhett Roberts, Marcus Harper, Anthony Vickers, and Eric Cook among others.

Another unsubstantiated rumor that Tara was involved with another student named Eric Cook. A friend of his had made mention of their affair in an Internet forum post where he stated that everyone knew that they were "messing around." He also said that the police didn't make the information public out of respect for Tara's family as she dated around quite a bit. An alleged friend of Cook disputed the rumor on the forum, however. Cook would later die in a car accident.

A neighbor, Joe Poirier lived with his wife and was rumored to have been "obsessed" with Tara. The older couple admitted to "looking out for Tara" and they were fond of her. He was seen pouring concrete near his home the day after she disappeared.

Another person of interest was Larry Gattis, the brother-in-law of Tara. He was brought in for questioning after the disappearance. It would later be revealed that he had been asked if he had an affair with Tara.

Larry answered 'no'.

The polygraph machine marked it as a 'deceptive answer.'

48 HOURS

In 2008, Tara's case would be featured on the CBS News show "48 Hours Mystery." The show would illustrate the parallels between Tara's case and the disappearance of Jennifer Kesse who would go missing in Orlando, Florida three months later. The GBI would also reveal during the broadcast that they had found a latex glove in Tara's yard just a few feet away from her front porch.

The GBI forensic team would analyze the DNA left in the glove and determine that it was a man's DNA, they just do not know who it belongs to. They would compare the DNA samples of the numerous men who were associated with or knew Tara but none of them have matched.

The DNA has also been entered into the Georgia and national databases but no match has been made to date.

"The glove may be a red herring," Orange said. "Whoever entered the home left nothing behind, no prints, DNA, nothing. So it was obviously someone who knew exactly what they were doing. They wanted to harm Tara."

A HOAX AND FALSE TIPS

In February of 2009, a man calling himself the "Catch Me Killer" began posting videos boasting that he had murdered sixteen women. One of the women he described had a close resemblance to Tara Grinstead. The man producing the video digitally obscured his face and voice but police eventually identified the culprit as twenty-seven-year-old Andrew Haley.

Haley performed the videos as part of a bizarre hoax and was eliminated as a possible suspect.

Investigator Gary Rothwell has expressed his lament at how the rumors and speculation have caused unfair stress to many who have been already tried in the public eye. "Irresponsible public accusations have been made about them, and they have no way to respond or defend themselves. And it's frustrating that we don't have evidence to rule anyone in or out."

Rothwell admits, however, that he has information that has not been released.

In February of 2015, authorities acted on a tip which led them to drain a pond in Fitzgerald, Georgia.

They didn't go into details as to what the specifics of the tip were. The pond would be drained and nothing would be found.

ALIBIS

Police have alibis from all the men who knew Tara Grinstead but no one has been ruled out because no one can account for the full thirty-four hour period.

Rhett Reynolds stated he went to sleep after the cookout. Joe Poirier was with his wife next door.

The most elaborate alibi, however, came from Marcus Harper.

Again, Marcus was in a local bar and a friend of Tara's had spotted him there. She would call Tara at around 10:15 and 10:30 to tell Tara that Marcus was there.

After 1 am, Marcus left the bar and went to look for his police officer friend, Sgt. Sean Fletcher. Fletcher was on duty that night.

Fletcher knew Tara as well. Ironically, he was one of the officers who arrived at Tara's house when Anthony Vickers, Tara's former student, was banging on her door.

There were rumors that Tara didn't like Fletcher because he had told Harper that Tara was entertaining Heath Dykes at her home.

Fletcher would deny that speculation.

"What we can extrapolate from this scenario was that Vickers was angry that his crush, Tara, was with another man," Orange said. "So he goes to her home and demands that she talk to him. He's young, twenty-years-old, and doesn't understand why she would do this to him. He is then arrested by Fletcher who relays what Tara is doing to Marcus, a man that Tara is wary about because of his temper. So now we have more than just a love triangle, it is a love octagon, with numerous men vying for and getting jealous over the attention of Tara."

At around 1:49 am, Fletcher received a call from dispatch informing him that Marcus Harper was looking for him. The two met up and walked Fletcher's beat, checking doors in downtown Ocilla.

Around 2:45, Fletcher was dispatch to a home where a mentally unbalanced man, Bennie Merritt, had stumbled into a home and refused to leave. Marcus would join Fletcher on the call as did two other officers. Merritt, however, was gone from the premises.

Minutes later, they began to search for Merritt who was also a neighbor of Tara's. The drunken Merritt would accost the cashier at the local gas station then be apprehended. Both Fletcher and Harper had responded to the call at the gas station and by the time they were done it was 4:28 am.

Marcus then headed home.

Investigators would later be able to corroborate these details with multiple witnesses, including Merritt, who was scrutinized as a possible suspect in the kidnapping as well.

Marcus Harper, however, has not been ruled out as a potential person of interest in the case.

"Marcus's alibi is too perfect," GBI investigator Maurice Godwin said.

Both Larry and Anita Gattis believe that Marcus is the top suspect.

"He had the motive," Tara's sister said. "And the training."

The insinuation would draw the ire of Marcus who became upset that Anita consistently brought up his military and police training. He continues to deny any involvement in Tara's disappearance.

"I don't wanna hurt any innocent civilian much less someone I spent five and a half years of my life with."

"What is clear is that there isn't a whole lot forthcoming about Tara's personal life to draw the conclusions we need to about who is the most probable suspect," Orange said. "Like in the Natalee Holloway case, the sexual activity of the woman in question is kept hidden. If her background reveals that she was a promiscuous woman, there will e less sympathy and urgency to solve the crime. That is one of the more striking aspects of the case, aside from Tara's vanishing, is the cover-up of Tara's personal life in order to protect her reputation."

UNSOLVABLE CASE?

Tara Grinstead's case is still being investigated. The GBI reports that they receive numerous leads per day, most of which are false.

Her body has never been found but her impact on the lives of those around her and her students will never be forgotten.

"I'm so sorry to hear about what happened to Miss Grinstead," said Christine Kang, a South Korean exchange student from Grinstead's class. "She is so caring and giving to her students. I am sure she will come home soon safely. I will pray for her every night."

MURDER IN TEXAS : THE TRUE STORY OF RHONDA JOHNSON & SHARON SHAW

JAMIE FOSTER

Rhonda Johnson and Sharon Shaw were two teenage girls murdered in 1971. But despite having had their lives taken so long ago, their case is still not satisfactorily solved. It's a story that involves not just two girls being murdered so young, but a potentially innocent man imprisoned for over twenty years, a corrupt police force, a serial killer, and perhaps the wider context of the Texas Killing Fields murders.

The story of the twists and turns involved in finding justice for the two girls continues on until today. Michael Lloyd Self, the man who some believe to have been wrongly imprisoned for the murder of the two girls, has since died in prison of cancer. Because of his passing, and the difficulty that investigators have found in unearthing new evidence, it seemed unlikely that the full story will ever come out.

But not long ago, a revelation and a startling confession have brought Johnson and Shaw's murders back into the limelight. Perhaps, at last, their families can discover the truth of their real killers.

Who were Rhonda Renee Johnson and Sharon Shaw?

Sharon Lynn Shaw was born in Mobile, Alabama to Hoyt Shaw and Mary Ann Collins on August 11th, 1957. Rhonda was born in Houston, Texas to Charles Johnson Sr. and Betty Huey on December 16th, 1956. Not much is known of their early lives, although by 1971 they were living next to one another in Webster, Texas, and were good friends.

Both girls had finished with school for the year and were enjoying their time off together. The day of their disappearance began like many others that summer, with a day out on a pleasant morning. It was August 4th, 1971 and Johnson and Shaw wanted to take a day trip to Galveston, to Wix Ski School, and to visit Doug's Surf and Dive Shop which was nearby. The area also had a Dairy Queen and a popular swimming school, making it very popular with the teenagers of the surrounding area. Given that it was summer, the girls would most likely have preferred to stay all day, but had promised their parents that they would be home by 1pm.

They hitched a ride with a family friend, who took them on the 30 mile journey to Galveston. Unfortunately for the girls' parents, that morning would be the last that they would ever see of their children.

The afternoon came and went, and the girls didn't call home to explain their absence. After they missed dinner that night, their parents began to call their friends to see if they'd heard from them, and called the neighbor who had given them a ride. None of their friends had heard a thing, and the last their neighbor had seen was when the girls had been dropped off at the skiing school and surf club. The girls were soon reported missing by their parents, who went in person to the local police department.

According to Raymond Wix, the owner of Wix Ski School, the girls didn't stay long there that day. In conversation with the Webster Police Department, he had told them that they had headed off after being told that the ski boats weren't running that day due to choppy waters. That was the last that we can say with certainty about the girls' day.

It was in August that the pair crossed paths with the man who would end their lives, but it wasn't until the beginning of 1972 that the girls' bodies were found. Just after the New Year, two young men went fishing near Webster, Texas, their hometown. They came across a skull floating in the marsh, and one of the men wrapped it up in a towel, stowed it away and took it home. After sharing their find with the Harris County Sherriff, the skull was eventually identified as belonging to the missing Rhonda Johnson.

This triggered a large scale search of Taylor Lake and the Bayou, which despite its size took until February 17th to find any more evidence. That day, another skull was found in a nearby drainage ditch, and soon more bones were found. They were identified as belonging to both girls.

Michael Lloyd Self tried and convicted

While the girls' bodies were discovered in early January, it was only in late May the same year that progress began on their case. The city council hired a new police chief that month, Don Morris, who brought with him a new assistant chief, Tommy Deal. Eager that they be seen to be doing something on such a large crime for a small town, the pair acted on a tip they'd received about local man Michael Lloyd Self.

Self was, admittedly, a sex offender known locally who had already been arrested multiple times in 'Peeping Tom' incidents. It was Morris and Deal themselves who visited Self at his place of work, a gas station, where Self was working night shifts at the time. They questioned him on the topic of the 'two girls'- the officers, of course, referring to Johnson and Shaw. Self, however, believed them to mean his estranged wife and new girlfriend, and having been confused went to the police station later that day to clear the matter.

Upon his arrival, he was again questioned about Johnson and Shaw, this time being shown their photographs and interrogated on his connection to them. Self admitted to recognising them, and unfortunately for him, that seemed to be enough evidence for the new chief: he was arrested then and there on the charge of their murders.

Since he was now officially detained at the station- he had, after all, only arrived voluntarily that morning- Self's interrogation could now begin in earnest. Morris and Deal claimed that their suspicions rested on evidence that they had obtained, and urged him to confess. According to Jerry Mitchell, another officer at the police station that day, Self appeared calm and rational throughout the early stages of his questioning, clearly expecting any second that the officers would realise they had the wrong man.

He continued to deny the crimes as the morning wore on, but according to Self, the interrogations became continually more threatening and violent. Morris held him up against the wall, jabbed him with his nightstick, and even threatened to shoot him were he to carry on denying the crimes. Finally, Self had had enough: he wrote out his confession. He would later claim that Morris told him what to write, even forcing him to rewrite his confession several times over, a claim echoed once more by Jerry Mitchell.

During his time in court, Michael claimed that his confession had been forced out of him by the two officers interrogating him. These concerns were quickly dismissed, since after all, which murderer doesn't deny the charges against them?

Self's Confession: Details and Inconsistencies

It is easy to see why a jury or a prosecutor might be taken in by the confession, were they to consider the case 'open and shut' and not give it enough thought. It is particularly detailed with regards to the murders. Self first describes how he picked up Rhonda as he saw her walking along the road, turning around to pick her up in his car. They then drove to the Nassau Bay Yacht Club, where Rhonda found her friend Sharon. He claimed that he provided them with beer, offered them marijuana which they declined, and drove around the Clear Lake area 'feel[ing] good and getting loud.'

As the night wore on, Self's version of events is that Sharon had been hanging out of the window 'hollering at everybody and shooting peace signs at them' as he drove. Since neither of the girls wanted to go home, he claimed they went down to Clear Lake where he tried to assault Rhonda, which she rejected. Since Sharon was out of the car, Self continued assaulting her, and at her continued protests he became angry and hit both Sharon and Rhonda over the head with a Coke bottle repeatedly until they were both unconscious.

He goes on to describe how he drove the girls to an abandoned, dead end road, stripped them of their clothes and dumped their bodies in the Bayou.

Reading back the confession that Self may or may not have been forced to write, it is at least easy to spot several glaring, obvious mistakes. Perhaps the worst is that according to his confession, Self disposed of the girls' bodies more than twenty miles from where they were actually found. Both of the girls were found with their clothes on, not stripped as Self had claimed. Even the method by which he confessed to having murdered Johnson and Shaw was incorrect according to the coroner's report, with Self claiming to have strangled the girls, but their bodies showing no such marks.

Moreover, Sharon's family dispute the confession since it mentions Self picking up the young girl from her family home, which they deny. The confession also states that Self and the two girls were in Webster at 9pm, whereas eyewitnesses disagree and place the two girls- alone- in Galveston instead. The written confession is even further discredited by Self's later verbal confessions, which contradict several key points. For instance, Self repeated his claim during a polygraph test taken three days after his initial arrest that he stripped the girls before dumping their bodies, when they were in fact found with their clothes on.

The story only continues to get stranger. Two weeks after Self was first arrested, while the officers were still building the case against him, he was actually taken from jail by two deputies. They had told Self that they were going to buy him dinner. In fact, they took him out of town to the locations which Self had mentioned in his confessions to take pictures of him as a sort of third and final confession. These photos were even presented in court as evidence.

This episode is mentioned in the court records of Self's appeal. There, the scene is painted as Self agreeing to show the two deputies the various locations involved in the murder. First, the group went to the Sizzler Steak House, where Self said he picked up Rhonda (contradicting his claim that he had picked her up on El Camino Real, a nearby street, where she had been walking). According to this testimony, after picking up Sharon they then went to a Jack in the Box restaurant. The fact that this confession had been so different to his previous one, however, did not constitute enough of a problem for either confession to be inadmissible according to the court records of Self's appeal case.

Time passes by

After Self's conviction, justice did appear to have been done. Trust in the police was higher than it is today; if a man had been arrested, tried, and convicted of a crime then the case was, quite simply, closed. Self, for his part, never gave in. He continually appealed the case and applied for parole, beginning taking the case to an appeals court just a year after his first imprisonment.

According to the court records, Self complained on several grounds. First, he claimed that the evidence presented at his first trial was 'insufficient to sustain his conviction', mostly due to his claim that his confession was forced, but also because the photos taken at the various locations relevant to the case shouldn't have been admitted as evidence.

Unfortunately, each time Self applied for parole, or put his case up for appeal, he was unsuccessful. In the eyes of the law there was little reason to overturn the ruling. Self's first confession did contain some errors, but was also correct on several points, particularly that the bodies were disposed of and found in water. At appeal, the judge decided that enough of the confession corroborated with material evidence to uphold the previous verdict.

While Self's protests had been dismissed, the case still seemed to some to be too flimsy to have justified the certainty of a seventy year sentence. Like many similar cases before his, Self's case was eventually dramatized as part of the TV show, Unresolved Mysteries. David Coburn, a local investigator interviewed in the episode, actually backed up Self's story of Morris' mistreatment of him during his interrogation. Coburn claimed that he had seen Morris' brutality first hand during another interrogation the year before. The show raised the same questions as Self had done, but of course left it to the viewer to decide as to whether he truly was guilty or not.

Morris and Deal's Motives: The Texas Killing Fields

The show also raised the question of why, exactly, Morris and Deal had been so eager to arrest Self on such little evidence. In all of their efforts to extract repeated confessions from the defendant, it certainly seemed that they must have had their reasons. First, Self was well known locally for his sexual misdemeanors. For the city, it would make their lives a lot easier to finally put Self away for a longer sentence. It also made sense for the new chief to make it obvious that he was hard on crime. A new chief not addressing one of the largest and most shocking cases in Webster history would certainly give a bad first impression.

Last, but certainly not least, is the fact that the area had seen an unnaturally large number of murders from the start of the 1970s, which we today call the Texas Killing Fields murders. If Johnson and Shaw really were victims of the same serial killer as the other murders in the area, they were some of the very first to be killed. However, by the time they were discovered, five other girls' bodies had been found in the local area.

Whether law enforcement at the time would have recognised that these murders were perhaps the work of a repeat killer, they would at least have been aware of the spate of local killings, and been desperate to pin the crime on somebody. This, perhaps, was part of the reason why Morris and Deal were more eager than they should have been to try to pin those crimes on Self. At the very least, newspaper clippings from the time of the investigation reveal the public concern over previous missing persons' cases, as well as the deaths of many other young girls from the area. In a copy of The Odessa American from June 10th 1970, the author reveals that Self was suspected to perhaps have had a hand in the many other recent local murders.

The two girls were far from the last victims, however, as the Texas Killing Fields murders continued through the 1980s and 1990s, some even coming after the turn of the century. Almost every victim has been between the ages of 12 and 17, and every victim has been a young girl or woman. In total, at least 30 bodies have been found all within a 25 acre area just off I-45. Even aside from the discovered bodies, many more local girls have gone missing and are featured on websites like The Charley Project, a site dedicated to tracking down missing persons. All of this has led some to believe that the murders must be the work of a serial killer.

They certainly fit the bill: all around the same area, the vast majority of the victims fitting the same description, and a relatively steady pace of killings through the years all suggest the work of one lone actor. The only real argument against the idea is the fact that the killer must somehow have remained at large for so long, despite leaving such an obvious trail. If the murder of Johnson and Shaw really were part of the Texas Killing Fields murders- and given that the murders were often of pairs of young girls around their age, it would seem very likely- then Self could not have been their killer, since the murders continued for long after he was incarcerated.

A Twist in the Tale

Whether the Texas Killing Fields murders were the acts of a lone serial killer, or how he must be innocent if Johnson and Shaw were two victims of that same killer, was irrelevant to Michael Lloyd Self. Despite all of his protestations, appeals, and parole hearings, he remained in prison. It was only in 1998 that any development in this seemingly long-dead case came about. Edward Harold Bell was already in prison, after a manhunt that spanned the globe. He had been on the run since 1978, after the attempted assault of a group of children and the murder of a Marine, Larry Dickens, who had attempted to intervene.

The murder was especially brutal. It had taken place in a normal, suburban street; Bell had been coasting around in his car, searching for girls. Finding a group of young teenagers, he had stopped his car and jumped out, not wearing anything below the waist. Dickens, a local resident, noticed what was happening and attempted to intervene. Unfortunately for him, Dickens didn't like being interrupted.

He went back to his car, picked up a pistol and began shooting. Larry struggled back to the garage, where his mother had been watching the scene, and collapsed in her arms. Bell didn't stop shooting. When he ran out of bullets in his pistol, he went back to his truck to exchange it for his rifle, and carried on.

Bell would have been guaranteed life in prison for the brutal murder, but skipped bail and went on the run for 15 years. In 1984 he be was identified as part of a failed burglary in Texas, but still managed to avoid the police before finally being tracked down in Panama in 1993. Upon his eventual capture, he was finally convicted of the murder of Dickens and received 70 years in prison. Bell's murder of Dickens, too, was featured on Unresolved Mysteries; curiously, Matthew McConaughey caught his first big break on TV playing the role of Larry.

His connection to the Johnson and Shaw case was completely unknown before he confessed not just to their murders, but to the murder of eleven girls in total in the 1970s. The frankly disturbing letters were sent to prosecutors for both Harris County and Galveston County way back in 1998, but were kept under wraps until 2011. The letters initially claimed a tally of seven lives, but in interviews with the Houston Chronicle after their publication admitted to the total of eleven murders. In them, he claimed to have been a part of a government brainwashing program that forced him to assault, rape, and kill young girls.

Who Was Edward Harold Bell?

According to the Houston Chronicle, Bell had a 'normal' early life, 'even exemplary'. A boy scout who went on to earn a degree from Texas A&M, he made his living first as a licensed diver- where he met his wife- before settling as a travelling pharmaceutical salesman in West Texas. On the surface, he seemed like a normal man, with a normal job, and a happy wife and family.

According to Bell himself, however, his childhood was not idyllic. His family were always on the move since his father worked as a gauger at small oil fields across Texas, earning plenty of money to provide for his wife and son but forcing them to live an itinerant lifestyle. Not just this, but Bell also claimed that his father was excessively violent towards his family: in Bell's own words, 'My father thought if he beat you real bad, it would send chemicals into your bloodstream.' Bell fathered three children of his own over the years- but what his family didn't know was that he was leading a sordid double life.

Bell's crimes began much the same way as Self's had done: Bell progressed from peeping tom incidents, to masturbating in public and exposing himself to girls around Texas. According to the Chronicle, he was apprehended committing public indecencies at least twelve times, from Lubbock to Houston; his targets, teenage girls, often in pairs, but always unaccompanied by adults. More often than not, he managed to avoid prosecution or arrest for his actions. He began- at least, he was first caught- in 1968, exposing himself to teenage girls in the town of Sudan. Police and court records show that he continued on and off until at least 1978, the year he murdered Larry Dickens for interrupting an episode of his flashing.

Bell was in and out of mental institutions for a large part of that decade, on referral from court. He somehow didn't receive a single jail sentence for any of his sexual crimes, something which most likely wouldn't happen today. If he had been appropriately dealt with by the police for his previous crimes, the life of Larry Dickens could have been saved. In fairness to the police, however, his violent outburst was entirely unprecedented.

What Happened Next?

It would seem that at last, justice could have been done. Through all the years, Self had maintained his innocence, continued to claim that his confession had been forced, and that despite knowing the girls he had not been involved in their murders. Bell was a known murderer, already in prison, and provided remarkably accurate details with relevance to several missing persons cases in his letters. It would seem that given this detail, and Bell's prior crimes, that his confessions would force prosecutors to re-open the case and for Self's version of events, perhaps, to be reheard and finally believed.

All of this was not to be. As is so often the case with decades-old missing persons cases- in particular cases that seemed as closed as this- the new evidence wasn't treated with the interest it should have been. Astonishingly, Galveston County refused to present the letters to a jury for their consideration, and even worse, Harris County actually lost the letters altogether. Self remained in prison, unaware that a confession had even been made.

One of the prosecutors for Galveston County stated to the Houston Chronicle that he "...didn't believe we had sufficient evidence that we could proceed to grand jury with, and without getting into specifics, that's the decision that had to be made, no matter the temptations to proceed otherwise ... It wasn't for a lack of effort." In fairness to the prosecutors, the evidence to reopen a case of murder- particularly one that already, in the eyes of the law, has been settled- has to be very compelling, and perhaps the confession of a man known to be mentally unstable is not enough. After all, serial killers have been known to confess to crimes they may not have committed to gain infamy, or recapture the spotlight long after their conviction.

It was only two years later that Michael Lloyd Self died in prison, of cancer. If he really was innocent- and on the balance of probabilities, it seems that he may have been- then he will never see justice for his unlawful incarceration, which lasted a total twenty seven years before his death.

As for Bell, he remains in prison. He received 70 years for the inexplicably brutal murder of Larry Dickens, and so any sentence received for the murders of Johnson and Shaw- not to mention the other girls he claimed to have killed in the same letters- would be irrelevant. Bell was in his late 70s at the time of writing, and will die in prison.

The Johnson and Shaw cases are still, officially, the crimes of Michael Lloyd Self, and the case remains closed. Since Bell's letters were received by county prosecutors, no new evidence has come to light; the letters and accompanying information were not considered enough to reopen the case then, and aren't considered enough now. And due to Bell's refusal to co-operate with police, it seems unlikely that any new information on his potential part in the murders will ever be revealed.

THE DISAPPEARANCE OF KELSIE SCHELLING

ANA BENSON

Every time a woman goes missing or is found murdered, the police usually takes a closer look at their spouses or boyfriends. It is a standard procedure, especially if there were indications that they were in a troubled relationship. The disappearance of Kelsie Schelling is one of the biggest mysteries in Colorado. This young pregnant woman was last seen in February of 2013 and the case is still open to this day.

However, Kelsie's family was quite disappointed at the lack of interest by the police to investigate her then-boyfriend Donthe Lucas, who was clearly involved in this crime. After all, Donthe did invite Kelsie to his hometown on that fateful night and he was the last person who saw her alive. When they realized that the police are stalling with the investigation, the family made a promise that Kelsie's case will not be forgotten until they discover what really happened. They kept the public informed through their Facebook page and eventually managed to reach the Colorado Bureau of Investigation.

Early life

Kelsie Jean Schelling was born on 18th February 1991 in Holyoke, Colorado. She grew up in a tightknit family and later became even closer to her mother after the divorce of her parents. Kelsie was only eleven years old when they split up but she would often talk to her father as well. However, they didn't see each other that often because he moved to a different part of town. After graduating from high school, Kelsie attended Northeastern Junior College located in Sterling, Colorado. She was fascinated with psychology and planned to major in it once she gets accepted to the university.

Kelsie was friendly and outspoken, so it comes as no surprise that she had many friends and was a life of every party. During her time at Northeastern Junior College, Kelsie met Donthe Lucas. He was a star player on the basketball team and the two of them fell in love instantly. Donthe Lucas had a very difficult childhood and he grew up in Pueblo, Colorado which is an infamous place known for higher crime rates than anywhere else in the state. He loved basketball and it was clear that he would be an outstanding athlete even in high school. Basketball players do have enormous salaries so Donthe Lucas did see it as an opportunity to help his family out further down the line.

He was hoping that a scout would attend one of his games and recruit him for one of bigger colleges or universities that had a good basketball team. But his big break never happened. Instead, he ended up in Northeastern Junior College which was alright, but Donthe wasn't quite happy with that outcome. His dissatisfaction was evident even in the relationship with Kelsie. Their romance had constant ups and downs, and the two of them would break up, and get back together which drove Kelsie mad. They did finally call it quits after several semesters, and didn't see each other for quite some time.

After finishing the two years at the junior college, Kelsie pursued her education even further, and she moved to California to attend Vanguard University in Costa Mesa. She was finally able to study psychology full time. Donthe continued to play basketball for Emporia State University in Kansas. Kelsie's family was happy she managed to end her relationship with the troubled basketball player, and they hoped that she would make a new life far away from Colorado. Kelsie was independent and she enjoyed living and studying in California. When she wasn't attending classes, Kelsie worked at a tanning salon with her best friend. However, she did drop out of the college because the school work was a bit too much for her at the time and her only option was to go back home. She moved to Denver in 2012 and started working in a store. Meanwhile, Donthe Lucas was back in his hometown Pueblo.

The two of them started talking once again during the autumn of 2012. It was obvious that they still had feelings for each other, so no one was surprised when Donthe and Kelsie decided to spend the Christmas holidays together. The couple seemed happy to everyone around them, but Kelsie did tell her friends that their relationship was still very toxic. Donthe was still treating her badly, calling her names, and starting unnecessary fights. Soon enough everything will change. A few weeks after the holidays, Kelsie found out that she was pregnant. Shocked at first, Kelsie was lost and decided not to tell anyone for a couple of weeks. But keeping a secret was hard. So she called her mother and told her the news. Kelsie's mother Laura would later say that even though her daughter felt a bit stressed, she was still excited about the pregnancy. Yes, she was young but Kelsie was determined to make it work.

Donthe Lucas didn't take the news so well. Having in mind how dissatisfied he felt about his failed basketball career, it is not wrong to assume that the news about a baby simply solidified the fact that his dreams will never come true. Kelsie noticed the change in his mood and openly told him that he doesn't have to be a part of their baby's life. But it is also worth mentioning that Kelsie confided in her best friend that Donthe was ecstatic to become a father at one point. However, his mind was constantly changing. Kelsie went to see her doctor on 4th of February 2013 and he confirmed that she was eight weeks pregnant. The baby was healthy and doing well. The doctor provided her with an ultrasound of the unborn baby, and she was full of joy. Kelsie immediately sent out the pictures to her mother, her friends, and Donthe. Unfortunately, the excitement will not last forever.

The night of the disappearance

Donthe and Kelsey exchanged several emails on February 3rd, 2013. He invited her to visit him in Pueblo. She turned him down saying that she needs to go for a checkup the next day to make sure everything is alright with the baby. After seeing her doctor on the morning of February 4th, 2013, Kelsie went straight to the store. She worked the second shift and was expected to come home sometime after 10:00 PM that night. However, she was in contact with Donthe for the entire day, texting back and forth about the pregnancy. Donthe told her that she should drive out to Pueblo after work because he had a surprise for her. Not knowing what it is, Kelsie asked for more information because Pueblo is two hours away from Denver, and she would probably be tired after work. He insisted that she would be happy with his surprise and that he cannot tell her anything over the phone.

It is safe to assume that Kelsie thought that Donthe was ready to change and start a family with her. Their relationship wasn't a standard one but it seemed like Kelsie was willing to move past all the negative things and focus on the future. So after her shift ended, Kelsie got in her Chevy Cruze LTZ and drove to Pueblo in the middle of the night. Donthe was supposed to meet her in a parking lot in front of a local Walmart. The surveillance cameras did confirm that Kelsie got there on time, but Donthe was nowhere to be seen. She waited in a parked car for almost an hour before sending another text message to Donthe, saying that she has been in the parking lot for too long and that she would come pick him up at whatever location he is at the moment. She got a reply sometime around 12:15 AM.

Donthe told her that he will be waiting for her in the street next to his grandmother's home. Kelsie is seen exiting the parking lot a couple of minutes after she got the message. She clearly did arrive at the second rendezvous spot, but once again Donthe wasn't there. Kelsie sent him another message asking where is he and Donthe replied that he will be there in a minute. This is the last known communication between these two until sometime before 04:00 AM. After going through the phone records, police did discover that Donthe called Kelsie at 03:54 AM but she didn't pick up. The significance of this mysterious phone call will be revealed later. After reviewing the cell tower pings for both phones, the investigators did discover that they were in close proximity to each other.

The search for Kelsie

Kelsie's mother Laura got really worried the next day because she wasn't able to reach her daughter over the phone. She tried calling numerous times but it went straight to the voicemail. The last message she got from her daughter was the ultrasound image of her unborn child, and Laura wasn't sure if something happened to Kelsie after work, or she was ignoring her calls. Laura contacted Kelsie's friends who told her that she went to Pueblo to meet with Donthe. With no word from her daughter, she called Donthe who picked up his phone and told Laura that he had seen Kelsie last night, but that she drove back home in the morning.

Laura was starting to panic, but she did tell Donthe that she would involve the police if she doesn't hear from her daughter soon. Laura and Kelsie were very close and they did tell each other everything, but she suspected that her daughter kept this information from her because she didn't want Laura to know that she was meeting with Donthe. After all, Laura was aware of the nature of their relationship, and his reluctance to accept the baby. Plus, Laura would probably advise Kelsie not to go to Pueblo in the middle of the night.

Laura contacted the local law enforcement and told them that her daughter was missing. Without any solid leads or evidence, they started asking around for Kelsie. Their first step was to take a closer look at Donthe because he claimed that he was the last person to saw Kelsie. She did travel from Denver just to see him. After checking Kelsie's credit card records, they did notice that the card was used hours after Kelsie's last known contact with Donthe. They reviewed the surveillance of the ATM and noticed that Donthe had the card and picked up $400 from Kelsie's account. They weren't sure if Donthe had Kelsie's agreement to use the card, but that was a felony in the state of Colorado, so he was led to the police station for questioning. He had a lot of things to clear up, starting with the timeline of Kelsie's visit to Pueblo.

Donthe's interview

After being picked up by the police, Donthe told his own version of the story. They did see each other that night and talked until early morning hours. Donthe and Kelsie got into a fight and she felt too agitated to drive back home to Denver. She was also very tired from working the second shift. Instead, Kelsie decided to sleep in her car which was parked near his grandmother's house. According to Donthe, his phone rang sometime around 07:00 AM and it was Kelsie. She wasn't feeling well and asked Donthe to drive her to a hospital. He put on his clothes, got to her car, and drove her to the Parkview Hospital.

Kelsie wasn't sure if something happened to the baby during their argument last night and she insisted to see a doctor before she heads out to Denver. Donthe sat inside her car in the parking lot for two hours when she finally emerged from the hospital. Kelsie told him that she had lost the baby. She then asked Donthe to drive her to Walmart to get something to eat and buy some snacks for the road. The two of them started fighting while they were in Walmart and Kelsie refused to drive him home. Donthe simply walked away and got to his grandmother's house on foot. He didn't see Kelsie later in the day and he assumed she went home. He didn't mention stopping at the ATM to pick up the money during his initial interview.

The investigators did notice a couple of possible leads that could collaborate Donthe's story, namely the Parkview Hospital. Each medical facility keeps detailed records of the patients they treat. After speaking to the staff and going through the data, they have confirmed that Kelsie didn't check in during the morning of February 5th. There were also numerous surveillance cameras all over the building and none of them picked up Kelsie entering or leaving the hospital. It was obvious that this part of Donthe's story was not true.

Of course, the police investigators decided to check out Walmart as well because the parking lot and stores do have surveillance cameras, and they might have picked up something that would be of use. While they couldn't find Kelsie or Donthe entering the Walmart, they did notice Kelsie's car on the parking lot. However, the timeline didn't match up with Donthe's story because Kelsie's car appeared at noon, and not in the morning. Plus, Donthe was the only passenger in the car.

Another surveillance camera which was positioned on the back side of Walmart did record Donthe getting into his mother's car – another detail he failed to mention in the initial talk with the investigators.

Without any proof that Donthe's version of the events is true, they called him up for a second interview. The investigators did have a plan this time - they wanted to find out more about the ATM, and how it fits into his timeline. He told the detectives that he took $400 in order to pay his bills and that Kelsie lent him the money since he was at the ATM while Kelsie was at the hospital. When the detectives told Donthe that there is no record of Kelsie ever being in that hospital, his reply was: "I don't even know what to say right now."

They also presented him with Walmart surveillance video that proves Donthe was the only person in the car. He was surprised with the evidence put in front of him, and before the detectives managed to get him to open up, he decided to lawyer up. He was only charged with the identity theft due to the fact that he used Kelsie's credit card, but the case was dropped. The judge had determined that Donthe did use Kelsie's credit card in the past and it was a normal behavior. However, nobody managed to figure out why Donthe had her card in the first place. After all, if Kelsie decided to ran away and start a new life, she would need the money, as well as her vehicle.

Speaking of Kelsie's car, the investigators took a closer look at the surveillance video from Walmart parking lot because they wanted to follow the vehicle. Exactly one day after Donthe left Kelsie's car there, another man approached the car and got inside by using the key. He didn't break in or steal the car. The man was dressed in black, wearing a hoodie, so identifying him was almost impossible. His body type was different than Donthe's, and the mystery man was significantly shorter. Keep in mind that Donthe was a tall basketball player, so his height would be noticeable, even in a low-quality video.

Seeing the direction in which the car went, the police collected the surveillance videos from stores and businesses which were in close proximity. They put the puzzle pieces together and found a route but they couldn't follow it all the way. One day later, the car was dropped at the parking lot of Saint Mary Corwin Hospital. The man locked the car and walked away. The investigators located the vehicle on 14th of February, 2013 and figured out the timeline. But nobody knows where the car was during 6th of February. There weren't any signs of a struggle that would indicate that Kelsie was killed in her car. Almost all of her personal items were missing, including her wallet and a backpack.

While it is unclear if the vehicle was tested for the traces of DNA, an unnamed police officer who worked for Pueblo Police Department will later say that they did find bodily fluids in the trunk of Kelsie's car, as well as two palm prints. However, no one knows what happened with this evidence and was it ever tested. It is simply another thing which the police investigators decided to ignore in this case. Unfortunately, the whole investigation will be under scrutiny soon after.

Theories

Figuring out a solid theory without too many evidence or information can be challenging. Laura, Kelsie's mother, claims that her daughter was probably murdered and that it was premeditated. The first red flag for her was Donthe's initial invitation to meet him before the doctor's appointment. When Kelsie refused, he knew that he had to act fast. Donthe lured Kelsie to Pueblo by saying that he has something to show her, but he never gave an explanation to the law enforcement about what the surprise really was.

It is clear that Kelsie was alive and well up until the point she met Donthe in the street next to his grandmother's house. This is where the trail goes cold. The activity on her phone stops until 04:00 AM. If we analyze the location of the phones, another theory is that Donthe led Kelsie to a remote location and harmed her. It was possible that Kelsie dropped her phone in the middle of a struggle. Donthe couldn't find the phone in the dark, so he had to call her number. He was very likely getting rid of the evidence.

There is a possibility that the two of them did indeed get into a fight, and that an unfortunate accident happened. However, it is more likely that Donthe planned to get rid of Kelsie, and had planned every single step he would take that night. He really insisted to see her as soon as possible. While it is not fair to put the blame on the rest of Lucas family, the fact that his mother picked him up immediately after he left Kelsie's vehicle at the Walmart's parking lot indicates that she knew what was going on. Pueblo Police Department did stop investigating Donthe, and they claimed they didn't have enough physical evidence to prove that a crime really occurred. But they did receive a couple of noteworthy tips which were ignored and never pursued.

The missed opportunities

The entire investigation of the disappearance of Kelsie Schelling was troubling from the very beginning. While the detectives did not have physical evidence of a crime, it was clear that Donthe was the last person who saw Kelsie alive. In every standard investigation, he would have been the prime suspect, and the investigators would do their best to find more proof that he was somehow connected to the crime. The cell tower pings did show that both of their phones were in a remote area next to Pueblo in the early morning hours.

But there are even bigger missed opportunities that could have provided the investigators with the proof they needed. For instance, Donthe was living in his grandmother's house at the time of Kelsie's disappearance. However, the entire family moved out soon after. The landlord started redecorating the house because he wanted to rent it again. He did hear about the missing girl from Denver but had no idea about the details of the case, or the fact that the Lucas family was involved in any way.

He decided to put the new carpets in and when he lifted the old one, the landlord noticed a strange stain on the bottom. He contacted the police enforcement because he was worried that something bad has happened in the house. However, the police ignored his request to check out the stained carpet, and no one had ever arrived at Lucas' previous residence to pick it up. The landlord ended up throwing the carpet away because he simply couldn't keep it forever in the house and wanted to move on with the renovation.

Another missed opportunity involved a couple of fishermen who were out on a lake on a night fishing expedition. It is important to mention that the lake was located near the Saint Mary Corwin Hospital. As you might recall, that was the spot where the police officers discovered Kelsie's vehicle on the 14th of February 2013. They were out on a bank when a hook got stuck to something poking out of the sand. The fishermen went to investigate and were sure that they saw a part of a human ribcage, as well as a skull.

They were terrified by that discovery and left the area right away. Both of them were reluctant to notify the police because they did have some troubles with the law in the past. But that didn't stop them from telling this story to their friends who urged them to contact the local law enforcement. A couple of months passed before they finally talked to the police, but the lake wasn't searched afterward.

The current searches

Family and friends continued to search for Kelsie even after it was clear that the police enforcement forgot about her case. They created a Facebook group that was constantly updated with new information. Pueblo Police Department did go through many changes after Kelsie went missing. The lead investigator was replaced with a new one who was willing to cooperate with the Schelling family. The Schellings did offer a large reward for any new leads that might help them locate their missing daughter. The reward was $100,000 at one point.

This eventually led to false claims and misleading messages such as the one which claimed that Kelsie was still alive, but was placed into a sex traffic ring after a hired hitman decided not to kill her.

Laura Schelling contacted the police and told them about the message. Since the investigators decided to follow every lead possible, they dug deeper and even involved the FBI. Their experts did manage to trace the message back to Russia through the IP address so it was clear that this tip was useless.

The biggest break in the case happened in the spring of 2017 when Colorado Bureau of Investigation finally got the authorization from the local law enforcement to join the search. CBI did determine that the prime suspect should be Donthe Lucas, and they got the warrant to search the area around his previous place of residence. A large number of police officers was seen around that house during April of 2017, and they dug up the parts of the backyard using heavy machinery.

The search has been successful and the officers left the scene carrying bags of evidence. However, they stated that they didn't find any traces of Kelsie's remains. Kelsie's family released the following statement after the search: "The past 2 days have been grueling and emotional, ending with the outcome we did not hope for. Kelsie is still missing. There is no way for me to convey to you all the pain that I feel right now. Sincere, heartfelt thanks goes out to the members of Pueblo PD, CBI and Parks & Rec who worked so hard on this search for Kelsie. This was a physically demanding excavation for them and we witnessed how hard they worked. Despite all the issues we have had in the past, the new leadership over Kelsie's case from PPD and active involvement from CBI is giving us hope that an effective investigation is finally taking place."

The case is still active and the police didn't arrest Donthe. But the positive changes are happening and Kelsie's family is certain that they will find the answers they are looking for now that the investigation is finally moving forward.

THE DISAPPEARANCE OF BRITTANEE DREXEL

86

FAITH TORINO

Brittanee Drexel disappeared from Myrtle Beach, SC while on spring break on April 25, 2009. She was 17 at the time and traveled without receiving parental consent. She told her mother that she was staying at a friend's house near their home in Rochester, New York. Brittanee's mother, Dawn, then learned where she really was when her boyfriend, John, called her after he suspected something had happened to Brittanee. Her parents immediately grew angry, scared, and devastated when they received word that their daughter was missing.

Brittanee was born on October 7th, 1991 and lived in Rochester, New York. She moved frequently during her youth as her father was in the military. She was a junior at Gates-Chili High school and the year was a rough one with her parents separating. She would live with her mother but still see her father frequently.

She was blind in her right eye and had several surgeries to correct her hyperplastic primary vitreous. To keep her eye from wandering, she would get contacts that made both eyes look the same.

Britt was described by friends and family as a smiling, fun-loving girl. Her demeanor had changed by her junior year in high school as she was depressed that her parents were separating. She would sleep in late and begin to skip school. She would overdose two times on her mother's pain medication and both times were fueled by the fact that she had just broken up with her on-again, off-again boyfriend, John Grieco.

"I felt it was all my fault," Brittany's father said. "When I was here none of this went on. She didn't ingest as many pills as they thought but still watching her get her stomach pumped was a warning. I need help."

"I remember the look on her face," Dawn said. "She was all red. She was crying, tears coming down her face. 'Why would you do this? Nothing in life is that bad.'"

Brittanee would be forced to see a counselor after the suicide attempt. Still, things seemed as if they were a mess on the home front.

Her parents were separating and her mother was losing her home. But she would resume her studies at school and excel on the soccer field.

"She was fast," her father said. "Her coach would say he'd never seen a girl that fast."

By the time Spring Break rolled around in, she was ready to go on an adventure with some of the older kids she knew. It was a long-standing tradition for Rochester students to go to Myrtle Beach for vacation. Britt wanted to enjoy the night life and lay out in the beach, so when one of her older friends asked if she wanted to come along she didn't hesitate.

She asked her mother first and the idea was immediately shot dawn. Dawn Drexel did not know any of the friends that would be taking Brittanee.

"She asked me and I said 'no,'" Dawn recalled. "Then she went to talk to her father. She would play us both. She would say Mom said 'no' but Dad said 'yes.'"

Brittanee was determined to go. She pleaded with her mother once again and was turned down. Angry, the two got into a fight and Britt would call her boyfriend to come pick her up.

Brittanee decided to fool her mother. She told her mother that she wanted to stay at a friend's house nearby for a couple of days. Dawn reluctantly agreed but Brittanee headed off to South Carolina instead.

Dawn believed that someone had offered her something, like a "modeling job or some other kind of ruse" to get her to go down there. She had aspirations of being a model as well as getting into cosmetology. With her striking good looks, she would be a shoo-in for success in the modeling profession.

"Her biological father was Turkish," Dawn said. "She had a very European look."

Defying her mother, Brittanee would visit her boyfriend at his workplace and tried to entice him to come along. The young man declined, stating that he had to work.

Brittanee then left with her older friends Jennifer Oberer, Phillip Oberer and Allana Lippa to Myrtle Beach. Jennifer was twenty-one years old. Her brother Phillip would be charged with rape in an unrelated case (charges would be dropped) in 2010. It is believed that these were considered the 'cool kids' and that Britt wanted to hang out and be liked by them.

Britt texted her boyfriend numerous times throughout the trip, telling him about the ambience. She expressed her love for the hot weather, palm trees and the happy vibe of young people finally away from parental supervision. But according to friends and family, Brittanee didn't know the older kids that well.

She also called her mother and lied, telling her that she waswatching movies at a friend's house.

CHANGE OF HEART

Britt hit the clubs with her friends and her mood quickly changed. Her friends began using a lot of drugs and she didn't want any part of that scene. She went off by herself, checking out the local shops and walking down the beach.

She then met up with a friend from Rochester, a man named Peter Brozowitz. He was also in town and staying at the Blue Water Resort with his own group of friends; Matthew Abrams, Philip Watson, Keith Cummings, and Anthony Schimizzi. The 20-year old Brozowitz was a "club promoter" who got Brittanee into Club Kryptonite. The next morning, she would meet Peter again at the beach.

The next day, Brittanee called her younger sister and told her that she's at the beach. Her sister believed she's at the local beach which is only twenty-minutes away. Britt then has a friend to impersonate the parent of the friend get on the phone to talk to her mother. The friend assured Dawn that everything was okay.

Britt then got back on the phone with her mother.

"I'll see you tomorrow," Britt said. "I love you and I'll see you tomorrow."

It would be the last time Dawn would ever speak to her daughter.

THE MYSTERY OF WHAT HAPPENED THAT NIGHT

Brittanee decided she would meet up with her friend Peter that night. She borrowed a pair of shorts from a friend and headed out. She texted her boyfriend John, telling him that she's having a miserable time and that she doesn't like the people she went down with. Apparently, they were 'mean-girling' her after she didn't do drugs with them.

She then received a text from her friend who stated that she wants her shorts back. Irritated, Brittanee walked back to the hotel to return the item.

At least that is what her friends say happened as Britt would disappear into the night.

John then became worried when Britt did not text him back. He texted her a few more times, waited, received no answer then he threatened to tell her mother that she's in South Carolina if she doesn't respond back.

Convinced that something is wrong, John calls Dawn at home. He explained that Brittanee is in Myrtle Beach.

Dawn went livid but her anger soon turned to concern when Britt didn't respond to her own texts or calls.

Everyone in Brittanee's family was notified. Something was wrong. Terribly wrong.

The next morning Dawn, her parents and John all made the trek to Myrtle Beach to try and look for Brittanee.

THE SEARCH BEGINS

Police in Myrtle Beach were notified and questioned the friends that Britt had been staying with. Their answers were all the same, they had not seen Brittanee since last night. Police also turned to Dawn, questioning her about Brittanee's state of mind.

Would she run away? Had she done this before?

There was no indication that Brittanee had motivation to do such a thing. Nor did they have any reason to believe she was doing a lot of drinking or drugs.

With no other leads, detectives turned their eyes on the last person to have seen Brittanee, Peter Brozovitz.

Peter would make an appearance on the Dr.Phil show and proclaim his innocence. He stated that they were in his hotel room watching the Yankees-Red Sox game when Brittanee was engaged in a texting argument with Jen Oberer who wanted her shorts back.

He said she didn't have a problem with walking a mile back to her own hotel.

Brittanee's parents were on the show and berated Peter for not "being a gentleman" and driving her back to the hotel. They also found it suspicious that Peter and the rest of Brittanee's friends did not do more after she was missing.

"I had spoken with Peter that morning," Dawn said. "He was giving me three different scenarios...It's fishy."

Peter responded angrily, stating that he was 'being thrown under the bus.' The innuendos were clear, that even if he had nothing to do with Brittanee's disappearance, she went missing because he didn't look out for her.

What is suspicious is that Peter had abruptly left Myrtle Beach with his friends around 2 a.m, five hours after Brittanee had vanished. They left clothing behind in their hotel room and looked to have been in a rush.

Upon his return to Rochester, Peter hired a defense attorney.

Peter had told investigators that she left his room shortly upon arrival to return the pair of shorts to her friend. The detectives got a hold of the surveillance camera from the hotel and verified Peter's story. At precisely 8:48 that evening she was seen leaving Peter's hotel to return back to her own hotel. She should have shown up on a traffic camera about fifteen minutes away but she never made it that far. She was abducted somewhere along that street.

Police continued to question Peter. The young man stated that one of his friends was told by his mother to return home immediately. This story was corroborated and law enforcement did not pursue the matter any further.

Instead, they now focused on Britt's cell phone.

Britt's last text message to her boyfriend was around 8:58. Ten minutes after she had left the hotel she texted "I'm packing and going to sleep probably."

This would be the last outbound message she sent as then John began texting her repeatedly with no answer back.

But the calls she received from John and her friends were pinged by her cell phone. Every time a friend called, her cell phone communicated with the nearest tower.

In looking at her cell phone records, she was moving southbound. The last ping was received at the Poleyard boat landing.

Fifty miles away from Myrtle Beach and two counties over.

Whoever abducted Brittanee knew exactly where they were going. The place was isolated, a rural country islet that only fishermen or locals would know about.

This was not the kind of place a seventeen-year-old girl would go to on Spring Break.

The investigators launched their search in the area that was about four miles in radius. Unfortunately, the terrain was treacherous. Alligators, wild hogs, snakes and biting insects the size of golf balls populated the area looking for their next meal.

Four-wheelers were brought in to keep the alligators away from the sniffing cadaver dogs. Investigators came to the site armed to shoot any wild hogs that came near.

"If her body is here," one investigator told Dawn in an ominous tone. "She would be eaten within six hours."

The search was frantic in the beginning but investigators seemed to lose hope after a few days passed. Britt's family returned home to Rochester with sunken hearts.

Brittanee's little brother chastized her friend upon their returning, stating "I thought you were bringing Brittanee back!"

Eight months later, police still had no promising leads. They would get an anonymous tip to check out an area a few miles north of the original search area near the Scantee River.

Once again, they came up with nothing. But a couple out fishing found a pair of sunglasses that looked as if they would belong to a teenage girl.

Neither her parents nor her boyfriend recognized the sunglasses as belonging to Brittanee. A DNA test was performed on the glasses and nothing was found.

Her mother continued to believe that she's alive.

"I think she was taken and held against her well," Dawn said. "I think she has become the victim of human trafficking."

Investigators and reporters shot down the notion, however. Typically, human trafficking occurs where the victim has a language barrier and Myrtle Beach was not exactly a hot bed for that type of crime. The police did not rule it out but it is low on their list of possibilities.

From 1997 to 2010, South Carolina has reported 12 cases of documented sex tracking. All were women, according to Doors to Freedom, an organization that helps victims of sex trafficking.

A few months later, police would receive some cell phone footage of Brittanee shot by a young man she had met. There were a group of teens antagonizing her and she wanted the young man's help to hang out with her so they would stop. He shot some footage of her sitting by herself, texting her boyfriend. He has since been cleared of any suspicion as he did have an alibi.

Pressed for suspects, law enforcement looked at every possible lead.

Three years later, authorities identified fifty-one year old Raymond Moody as a person of interest. They obtained a search warrant for a Georgetown motel room where Moody rented out at the time of Brittanee's disappearance. They noted that Moody had received a traffic ticket in Surfside beach just one day after Brittanee went missing.

Moody was a a registered sex offender, having raped a nine-year old girl in 1983. He was released in June of 2004. But Moody did not cooperate with investigators and remained tight-lipped under interrogation.

He is also a suspect in the case of Crystal Soles who disappeared in January of 2005.

"We've heard his name before," Dawn Drexel said. "It's a possibility the cases are connected. We don't know what happened to Crystal or Brittanee."

Moody lived in an area where Brittanee's cell phone last pinged. He was referred to as "Mr.Clean" because of his resemblance to the bald character in the Mr. Clean commercials. He has not been mentioned in any police reports since 2012, however.

The FBI would get involved and offer their belief that Brittanee was abducted and taken to a "stash house" where she was raped and then murdered. Her body was then wrapped in plastic and she was thrown into an alligator pit where her body would presumably be eaten.

This narrative was offered by FBI Agent Gerrick Munoz who obtained the informaton from an inmate named Taquan Brown. Brown is serving a 25-year sentence for a different case but stated he was present during Britt's last moments.

He said he had seen Britt when he visited a "stash house" which was a moniker used by drug dealers to describe a place where they stashed weapons, money or drugs.

Brown stated that Taylor picked Britt up in Myrtle Beach and took her to McClellanville. Once there he "showed her off, introduced her to some other friend that were there...they ended up tricking her out with some of their friends, offering her to them and getting a human trafficking situation."

The stash house was in the McClellanville area, the last location where Britt's cell phone was pinged.

Brown told the officials that he saw Da'Shaun Taylor, who was 16 years old at the time, and several other men "sexually abusing Brittanee Drexel."

Brown then claimed he went to the backyard to give Da'Shaun's father money.

During this time, Britt tried to escape. She was caught by one of the men who "pistol whipped" her across the head. She was then taken back inside the house.

Brown stated that he heard two gunshots and then saw the woman being wrapped up and removed from the home.

The FBI agent revealed that "several witnesses" have told him that she was dumped in a pond that was filled with alligators.

Taylor has since been convicted of robbery in 2011 and could face a life sentence. He stated that he knows nothing of Britt's case and with the lack of evidence he has not faced any charges in her disappearance.

Chad Drexel, however, thinks Taylor may have been involved.

He recalled a time when he was out handing out Brittanee's missing person fliers and handed it to Taylor who was in his car.

"I gave him the flier," Chad said. "He had a car full of brothers, friends. He handed the flier to one guy in the back seat. They all laughed and then drove away and threw the flier out the window."

"I got mad. I said 'There's something about this guy...'"

After the information was released to the public, Taylor's mother, Reverend Joanne Taylor, immediately defended her son.

She stated that he had already served his time for the robbery (a McDonald's restaurant) and that he was a "great kid" that was only

16 years old at the time of Brittanee's disappearance. During her son's hearing, Taylor's mother took the stand and said the following:

"And I want to say that at the time of this alleged abduction, he was 16 years old. I was never a mother thatwould let my kids run loosely, and definitely not with the father, you know, out to do things. I kept great hold on him. I am a pastor of a church. They were in church, they had a strict bedtime, I knew every place that they went. MyrtleBeach would not be a place that he would go at the age of 16. So I just, you know, I ask for your fairness, I ask for, you know, the correct justice in this case. And know that he is not a flight risk. I mean, I teached them good values, I instill in them what few things that have happened, they have exemplified overall what I've taught them. He is not, you know, a flight risk or anything.

Chad Drexel read the testimony and immediately took to his own Facebook page.

I would like to set the record STRAIGHT with a STRONG REPLY to Joan Taylor's comments to the Post Courier in South Carolina this past Friday.

Based on evidence the FBI and the Myrtle Beach Police department has gathered, along with FACTS and SPECIFIC INFORMATION gathered from a team of Private Investigators that I HIRED to work with local law enforcement actively during the case (which will SOON COME TO LIGHT) – we have no doubt Timothy Da'Shaun Taylor played a significant role in the abduction and murder of my daughter.

Of course the mother of Timothy Da'Shaun Taylor is going to defend her son – as a father I can understand a need to defend your children. What I DON'T understand is defending your children when you must KNOW the truth.

Her assumptions and words stated have been verified INCORRECT and couldn't be farther from the TRUTH. We know Timothy Da'Shaun Taylor was witnessed by others (Witnesses NOT IN JAIL) with my daughter – we are just praying that they do the RIGHT thing and stop forward with what they know. Additionally he has been seen and followed to the EXACT area where my daughter's DNA was found. Joan Taylor claimed that the FBI and government are falsely accusing her son because of witnesses IN JAIL?! Well, we have other specific evidence, that I can NOT disclose at this time for the safety of my daughters case, which corroborates these testimonies!! Timothy Da'Shaun Taylor is KNOWN to be involved in dog fighting, bringing drugs to parties, and raping women (mostly Caucasian young women) he either picks up UNWILLINGLY or friends of friends that end up being drugged and taken there. This IS ONLY THE BEGINNING!! There is a TON more "EVIDENCE and HORRIBLE INFO" we would like the PUBLIC in that area be aware of for their safety, but we are unable to disclose at this time.

WITHOUT A DOUBT ....Timothy Da'Shaun Taylor is a suspect in my daughter's Disappearance and Murder! My family and I will be following the FBI's requests to keep specific details in our daughter's case under wrap until THIS HORRIBLE PIECE OF TRASH goes to Prison for Life. After the guilty verdict, we will be happy to dispel these fairy tales that are being spun by Timothy's family. It is disgraceful the way this FAMILY and their FRIENDS are supporting and claiming innocence of a "PROVEN"

FELON without even looking at the evidence presented and the FACTS surrounding the case.

Also adding this PIECE OF TRASH photo so everyone can see WHO HE IS!

On March 25th, 2017, FBI agents called Dawn Drexel to inform her they may have located Brittanee's remains. They are now searching an area 45 miles north of their previous search spot.

After two days, however, they gave up the search.

The case is ongoing.

MISTY COPSEY

Misty Copsey was fourteen years old when she disappeared on September 17th, 1992 after a trip to the Puyallup Fair.

Her case remains a showcase of administrative screw-ups and dropped balls. She was initially thought of as a runaway before foul play was finally suspected a month after the fact. Subsequently, there have been at least five people suspected of committing her abduction.

But the Puyallup police did not get within sniffing distance of Misty or charging anyone with her disappearance. Three different police chiefs and numerous detectives all took a swing at the case and whiffed. No one in law enforcement has been able to answer the question on everyone's lips.

What happened to Misty Copsey?

A GOOD GIRL

Misty was born in 1978 to Diana and Paul "Buck" Copsey. Her father was a firefighter but the couple split up shortly after she was born and Misty lived with her mother.

Misty got good grades in school, excelling particularly in Math. During her last quarter at Spanaway Lake Junior High School, she got A's and B's. Athletic, she played softball, volleyball, and basketball before breaking both forearms during an athletic practice.

Misty was not the ringleader of a bad crowd. She was diffident but funny, entertaining her friends while skipping around and singing the theme song to Sesame Street.

She did not have much in regards to material wants. Her mother eked out a living as an in-home care nurse and they lived in a mobile home park until she was fourteen. Seeking a better place to live, Diana and Misty moved into a duplex where she now had her own room. But Misty longed for her friend who lived in and around the old trailer park. She would make it back there when she could to just hang out.

Tall, blonde and with green eyes, Misty was cute enough to draw the attention of boys. She remained chaste, however, and was not dating like so many of her other friends.

Her innocent, girl-next-door looks would draw the attention of Rheuban Schmidt. Rheuban looked like a casting call actor for a meth head. He sported a reverse mullet, a hairstyle that was cut close to the sides with curls on top. He had beady, green eyes that screamed low IQ. One of Misty's friends described him as a "scuzzy looking dude" but he nonetheless befriends Misty, much to the chagrin of her mother.

Diana grew suspicious of the relationship as Rheuban was four years older and a high school dropout. On one occasion, she listened in on the other end of a phone conversation Misty was having with Rheuban.

"I get horny just looking at you, Misty," Rheuban said, whispering like an old pervert.

Diana became enraged and ordered her daughter off the phone.

"Don't ever talk to that idiot again...."

ENTER CORY BOBER

Cory Bober was a thorn in the side of police every since the Green River killings became a national news story. He would insist that the police are "incompetent fools" while organizing his own searches for her remains. Diana would later accuse him of killing her daughter but he would respond by telling Diana that she was being "ungrateful." He was, after all, the only man on the case.

Bober was a recluse without a vehicle or a drive's license. An inveterate marijuana user, he had a record for both possession and dealing. He was also obsessed with cases of murdered or slain women in his home state of Washington. He had a stack of binders with autopsy reports, pictures, and other arcane details.

Bober came under the radar of the police in Puyallup when he became obsessed with the Green River Killer case. He had a brief acquaintance with Randall Dean Achziger, remembering a conversation where the man told him that the killer inserted rocks into the remains of his victim. Bober became suspicious as that would turn out to be a piece of information only known to police. He then went on a one-man crusade to prove the guilt of Achziger. Bober would interview his ex-girlfriends, friends, co-workers and present all of this in an affidavit to the courts.

Achziger found it ridiculous and annoying.

So did the police.

The Green River Killer would turn out to be a painter named Gary Leon Ridgway.

Bober didn't give up, however. He knew Achziger was the guy.

Bober had his own theories about who was performing the killings. Some were wild and outlandish conspiracy theories. Others were spot on. He would notice that there were victims that "had disappeared on the very same date that others were discovered. Some victims seemed to almost 'commemorate' the deaths or discoveries of others; one would die on a particular date and another would disappear a year to the day later on the very same date."

The police dismissed his theories as the rantings of a crack head. But Bober would be willing to show the proof of his connect the dots calculations. He pointed to the cases of Kim Delange, a 15-year-old killed in 1988 and Anna Chebetnoy, a 14-year-old killed in 1990. Both of their bodies would be found along Highway 410, east of Enumclaw.

Bober discovered that the remains of both girls were found in the same section of 410. The girls were found two years and one month apart. He felt that the killer was following a pattern.

He called the police department and left a voice mail. He predicted that a teen girl from Puyallup would disappear and her remains would be found on Highway 410 in the same vicinity where the other girl's bodies were found. Bober gave him the name of the man whom he felt was the serial killer.

Randall Achziger.

But the police were now used to his calls and viewed him as a crank. A nutcake with a strange vendetta.

His prediction would be half-right, however.

There would be no body found on Highway 410.

But a teenage girl would disappear.

Her name was Misty Copsey.

A NIGHT AT THE FAIR

On September 17th, 1992, Diana told her daughter Misty and her best friend Trina Bevard to behave themselves. Misty had convinced her mother to let them stay out that night...free of any meddlesome adults. But Trina's guardian would not allow her to go without an adult driving them home.

Diana worked as a caregiver for a 97-year-old Alzheimer patient who could not be left alone. She would not be able to drive the girls home. But Misty checked the bus schedules and convinced her mother that they would be okay. There was a bus that left the fair at 8:40 p.m.

Misty then convinced her mother to lie to Trina's guardian, Marlene Shoemaker.

"No worries," Diana said to Marlene. "I'll bring them home."

She wanted to be the cool parent, different from the stuffy adults who forgot what it was like to be fourteen. If it meant telling a white lie so her little girl could have some happiness, so be it.

What was the worst that could happen?

Diana dropped the girls off and gave them one last warning.

"Get home safe."

It would be the last time she would ever see her daughter again.

THE PHONE CALL

A few hours later, Diana would then receive a phone call from Misty as she tended to her elderly patient. Misty told her that she had missed the bus but could get a ride from Rheuban Schmidt.

Diana, knowing what kind of unsavory character Schmidt was, adamantly refused. She told Misty to find someone else to give her a ride back. Misty had an electronic diary which she used to store phone numbers. She told her mother she would find someone trustworthy to call for a ride.

"You call me back when you find someone," Diana said.

"I will. I promise."

Diana would wait all night for the phone call.

In the ensuing hours, Misty would not call back.

Worried, Diane called home in the hope that Misty had gotten a ride without calling her.

No answer.

Diana didn't panic. She figured that Misty went home with that scumbag Schmidt and didn't want to get yelled out for disobeying her.

She's going to get yelled at either/or. All Diana wanted was for her daughter to be safe.

Her shift finally ended and Diana drove back home in a rush.

Upon entering her house, she called out for Misty.

Silence.

She went into Misty's room and saw that it had been untouched from the previous night.

Diana would call the police in a panic. She told them that her daughter had not come home from the fair. The dispatcher would tell her that the police could not do anything about it for thirty days as it "sounded like a runaway case."

Diana knew otherwise.

Trying to calm herself, she figured that Misty was with Trina, that the two of them would be okay.

She called Trina's home.

No answer.

She then began scorching the earth with phone calls.

She would call Rheuban but he told her that she called but he didn't have the gas to go get her. She then called numerous friends of Misty and her mother.

No one had seen Misty.

She called Trina's home again, got no answer, then drove out to her house. She then went to the police department and filed a formal report with the Pierce County's Sheriff's Department who handled runaways as opposed to the Puyallup Police.

MISTY'S MISSING

Misty's friend Trina called Diana after she came back from school. She told the frantic mother that she didn't know where Misty was.

"The last time I saw her, she was heading for the bus," she said.

Diana would call Rheuban again. She would get his roommate this time, James Tinsley.

Diana needed answers. She interrogated the young fifteen-year-old like a grizzled police detective. She asked if Rheuban had been home all night. James then told her that Rheuban and his uncle went to pick up Misty but that he wasn't home just yet.

Later, Diana would call back and Rheuban would tell her that his roommate got the story wrong. He went to a party instead and didn't pick up Misty. He didn't know where she was.

Diana pleaded for the police to do something. They dragged their heels and began talking to some of Misty's friends. "Just call if she calls," they informed them. "No one gets in trouble."

Diana printed fliers with Misty's picture. She plastered them in and around the fairgrounds while calling the media.

The one woman search team would yield no leads. Rheuban would stop by and ask if the police had found anything yet. Diana would then wait at the bus stop near the fairgrounds to inquire with different drivers on the route. She found one driver who said that he saw Misty. She had asked when the next bus to Spanaway was arriving. The driver said it wasn't and that he was done for the night. He gave her instructions on which bus to take but she walked away before he could complete his sentence.

AN ERROR OF JUDGEMENT

Among the many mistakes that the Puyallup police made in the investigation of Misty's disappearance was to make the assumption that she was a runaway. Why they didn't entertain the prospect that she could have been kidnapped and murdered gave the abductor precious time to cover his tracks.

The police came to this erroneous conclusion after they interviewed Misty's mother, Diana. They thought she was a liar and an alcoholic. They then interviewed a pair of Misty's classmates who really didn't know her that well or accompany her to the fair.

A series of cover-ups then ensued, as the police told the media Misty had been found (where they got that information remains a mystery) and made no further investigation.

Until Diana and the media started to make a fuss. The department had to save face and eventually one of the detectives believed that this was not a runaway case.

Misty's disappearance could not be ignored any longer.

Police would talk to the various fair workers and security guards. No one had recalled seeing Misty.

The police then turned to her family, interviewing and doing background checks on both Misty's father, Buck, and Diana.

Their impressions of the duo would support their initial theory that Misty runaway. Diana was an alcoholic with multiple DUIs and seven years prior she had been convicted of welfare fraud. Buck confirmed that his daughter and Diana would have their issues.

Carver then discovered that Diana had filed a runaway report on Misty a month prior to her disappearing.

Diana would later state that the report was wrong. She thought Misty had disappeared then found her in the bedroom. She was too ashamed to tell the police it had been a false alarm.

With the police questioning and media coverage, Misty Copsey was now the talk of her Spanaway Lake Junior High school.

Rumors would abound at the school, one of which came from Misty Matthews who said that Misty had called her from Olympia. Another student stated that she saw Misty at a Color Me Badd concert at the fair.

The rumors were enough to prompt Carver to remove Misty from the FBI's National Crime Information Center as a missing person. He would once again treat her as a runaway.

BOBER'S THEORY

Cory Bober's knew he was right. He knew that police would find a body of a young woman off Highway 410.

He waited but nothing happened.

Until his mother showed him the flier of Misty's disappearance.

Right again!

Heart racing, he called the number on the flier. Bober would get into contact with Diana and hurriedly told her all about his research.

He talked about the Green River Killer, where and how he killed his victims. He would tell Diana that her disappearance was connected to the same guy responsible for the murdered Puyallup Girls, Kim Delange and Anne Chebetnoy.

Cory would apologize to Diana because he knew that Misty was dead. He predicted her body would be found somewhere along Highway 410.

The two would form an uneasy alliance. Bober became Misty's personal avenger. He would start a phone/letter/media campaign to prove the police wrong and himself right.

Misty was no runaway.

She was a victim of Randall Achziger.

In October, however, Bober would be arrested for selling marijuana. He was then accosted by Sgt. Herm Carver who tired of the young man meddling in police affairs.

"He walked in the room I was being held in – looking tired and pissed off. He said, 'I got out of bed tonight, and came down here to meet you – just to see what kind of a hypocrite you REALLY ARE!'

I said (being cocky), 'It's not MY FAULT – HERM – that you don't believe Misty Copsey's MISSING!!'

He yelled (angry), 'DON'T YOU EVER CALL ME BY MY FIRST NAME – IT'S SGT. CARVER TO YOU!!!'"

Bober's journals, November 1992

THIRTY DAYS MISSING

Sgt. Herm Carver and Deputy Brian Coburn would each individually warn Diana of the troublemaker that Bober was. Still, the worried mother would welcome his assistance as she needed all the help she could get. After numerous phone calls, the two would finally meet after a month of Misty being missing. Diana had nowhere else to turn but to the shaggy-haired twenty-six-year-old who lived with his parents.

The police were going through the motions on their end. Carver reactivated Misty's name on state and national lists but only because he was legally required to do so. At this point, he still believed Misty to be a runaway and doubted Diana's veracity.

Meanwhile, Diana would find Cory Bober's constant badgering to be annoying. It got so bad she filed a restraining order against him.

"My daughter has been missing for six weeks from the Puyallup Fair," Diana wrote in the restraining order. "Cory Bober has called me on a daily basis, telling me my daughter is dead. I was advised by Deputy Brian Coburn to file this complaint if I felt threatened."

The order would only last two weeks. Diana would then call the courts and rescind her request. She would later call Bober and apologize. Her daughter had been missing for over 56 days. Bober was annoying as hell but he was the only one doing research. The only one who cared.

Bober organized a volunteer search for Misty in the Green River area. He somehow coerced someone on the police forensic team to tell him the general vicinity of where one of the Puyallup girl's body was found. Bober surmised that Misty's body would be found in the same general area.

Seventy-two days after Misty had gone missing, there was now a volunteer team searching for her.

Nothing came out of the search.

But Diana would later spot Rheuban at a grocery store and confront him. The young man ran and got into a truck with an older man. She saw the look of fear and apprehension on both men as they sped off.

Diana would then lapse into a depression. She tried to commit suicide with booze and prescription drugs.

The next day she would wake up in a hospital. She would spend the next day there, drying out until being discharged back into the nightmare that had become her life.

A PLEA TO THE PUBLIC

Four months after Misty's disappearance, Diana would appear on a local TV station for a special on the Green River Killer. Jim Doyon, the homicide detective who worked the case, spoke of the killings but deferred on stating if Delange and Chebetnoy(the slain Puyallup girls) were connected.

Doyon took an interest in Misty's case. He would journey to Highway 410 and search near milepost 30 where the bodies of Delange and Chebetnoy had been discovered.

Like Bober and the volunteer search team, he too came up empty.

Bober was undaunted and organized another search. He realized that they had been searching in the wrong spot. They were searching on the south side of the highway when the should have been searching on the north.

Twelve people would show up for the search. Diana would arrive with her older sister, Debra. Bober would arrive with Al Hensley, the father of one of the slain Puyallup girls along with his 14-year old Boy Scout nephew, Jaremy Brown.

It would be the Boy Scout that would make the find

Poking into a ditch with his stick, he saw the crumpled blue jeans. Socks fell out of the jeans.

Baggy and stone-washed, they were cuffed at the bottom. The same jeans that Misty had borrowed from her mother on the night of the fair. The jeans were too big for her and Diana remembered them cuffing them on the bottom.

Bober became excited. He knew that the killer had planted the jeans there as a taunt.

He was right. The police were wrong.

But Diana, according to her sister, "broke into a million pieces."

THE KILLING FIELD

Seven dead women had been found in the nine-mile stretch between Enumclaw and Greenwater in the eight years prior to Misty's disappearance.

The two slain Puyallup girls were found in the same area in 1988 and 1991, only one hundred feet apart. They were left off a footpath that had been hidden by thick brush.

Both of the teenage girls had been presumed abducted from the Puyallup shopping center. Detective Jim Doyon believed privately that the cases were connected. He arrived at the site where Misty's jeans were found and interviewed witnesses, particularly Diana and Bober.

The jeans were taken to the lab and the forensic analysis indicated that the jeans had been in the ditch for some time.

Police suspected that someone (Bober? Diana?) had planted the jeans there.

What was undeniable that the jeans were found only a ten minute walk away from where the bodies of the two slain Puyallup girls were found.

SUSPICIONS ARISE

People began to talk. There were reporters who believed the jeans were planted there. Some were talking as if Diana and Bober were lovers and had plotted this for some insurance money.

Dede Miles, a fifteen-year-old friend of Misty, would come to Sgt. Carver with a tip. She said there was a boy that kept coming over to Misty's parties. He would always leave before her mother came home.

His name was Rheuban Schmidt.

Finally, the unkempt looking young man would come under the radar of the police.

Diana, meanwhile, began to suspect Cory Bober.

How did he know where to look? Why was this stranger so interested in the case to begin with? How did he know so much?

The police had warned her to stay away from him. Now she felt compelled to tell the police of her suspicions.

"Diana comes to station. Now feels Cory Bober may be involved in Misty's disappearance. I asked Diana to submit a written statement to that effect and why she feels he may be involved – she agreed to do so."

Carver's notes

AN INTERVIEW WITH TRINA

Detective Jim Doyon would interview the fifteen-year-old Trina Bevard, the last person to see Misty alive.

Six months had passed. Doyon had brought along the jeans with him, the sight of which made Trina cry.

"It seems to me like something that Misty was wearing that night," Trina said. "It looks very close to what Misty was wearing. The socks, they match what she was wearing. The jeans are big, so – her jeans were baggy that night, that she was wearing. They're – they were light blue like they are in the photo. It just seems, you know, it was the clothes that she was wearing."

Doyon would go on to ask what she was wearing (a pullover) and if she had any jewelry. He then asked if she had any cigarettes or birth control pills.

"No," Trina said. "She was straight. She was a virgin. She didn't smoke, she didn't drink, she didn't do drugs. She was clean, so she had no reason to do anything. She wasn't sexually active."

Trina then revealed that the girls made five calls to Rheuban. They could not get a hold of him. They finally got him on the line and he still refused to pick them up even when the girls offered him money. Misty told him about a key under the front doormat of her home. He could go inside, get money for gas and come pick them up.

Trina stated that she didn't trust Rheuban but only because he didn't keep his word and come pick them up. She then called a 23-year old friend named Mike Rhyner for a ride but they got disconnected. The girls were then stranded. They walked downtown to get to the bus stop before spotting a phone booth by a convenience store. Misty then called her mother, telling her that if Rheuban didn't come pick her up she would take the bus. The two argued as Diana didn't want Misty around Rheuban.

Trina had to get home by 10 p.m. She had about an hour and a half to get home which wasn't that far. Misty could not walk the ten miles to Spanaway.

Trina then decided to walk. She gave Misty her extra money for the bus.

"At that time I made my decision of walking home and she said she would take the bus," Trina recalled. "The last words that I said to her were 'Be careful,' and she turned around and told me the same and we walked off in different directions"

Trina also dismissed the notion of Misty being a runaway.

" Her mom just bought her a stereo and she was so excited and she went shopping and she got new clothes,"Trina recalled. She was telling me all about it. She was really excited about it.

BOBER GOES TO JAIL

Meanwhile, Bober would be sentenced to fourteen months in prison for the marijuana possession. He felt that the sentencing was too punitive and threatened law enforcement that they would never find Misty without him. His fellow inmates thought he was crazy and began calling him "snitch" and "The Green River Killer".

Jail would not slow down Bober's efforts, however. He continued to research and write Misty's mother.

"Dear Diana,

...When we found Misty's clothes, part of me died and I watched a part of you die too (much more than a "part") and I was at a total loss for words. I never wanted to be the one to show you your most horrible fears were true and that your daughter is truly dead at the hands of a sick murderer. I will never rest until the killer (Randy Achziger) is brought to justice and dead, if it takes my life to do it."

AMERICA'S MOST WANTED

Misty's case would eventually be broadcast nationally as it was featured on the America's Most Wanted television show.

Over twenty-eight tips came into Sgt. Carver from people who watched the broadcast.

When the tips went nowhere, Diana's suspicions returned to her original suspect, Rheuban Schmidt. She wanted Carver to speak to the young man but the Sergeant would take a circuitous route to get to Schmidt.

Carver would speak to Frank Rodriguez, the owner of Adam's Ribs, a restaurant where Rheuban worked. He convinced the owner to try and find out how much Rheuban knew about Misty.

"3-4-93 @ 1500: Frank states Rheuban said the following during a lengthy conversation about Misty Copsey:

- Yeah, I know about it.

- I know exactly where she is buried.

- They found the clothes but she is buried 6 miles from there.

- They're off by 6 or 6 1/2 miles."

— Excerpt from Carver's notes

Carver would then wait for Rheuban outside the restaurant before his shift started. Schmidt arrived, saw the cops and immediately ran off. The detectives would eventually catch up with him.

Rheuban would concede that he had received calls from Misty the night of her disappearance. But his story corroborated with Trina's, he told the girls he had no gas and could not pick them up.

Carver then asked if he knew where Misty was buried but Rheuban was adamant that he "said those things to get Frank off my back."

Rheuban then revealed that he suffered from "black outs". He stated that he did not recall anything until the daylight hours of September 18th, 1992.

The detectives pounced, asking if it was possible that he blacked out, picked up Misty and harmed her.

Rheuban claimed he didn't know.

All he knew was that he drove out to his grandmother's farmhouse and couldn't recall why.

Detectives would then give Rheuban a polygraph test.

They would later state that the suspect "zoned out" during the test, nearly falling asleep. The tests were inconclusive but detectives felt as if he were trying to beat the test.

A LITTLE LIE

Rheuban fell off the detective's radar when Carver talked to Dede Miles again. Dede would tell the detective that Trina had not walked home from the fairground like she told him.

Dede said that Trina had a boyfriend come pick her up and didn't want anyone to know.

Trina's boyfriend's name was Michael J. Rhyner. He had nothing on his record aside from traffic stops but he had friends that were connected with Chebetnoy and Delange.

He also had a complaint when he was sixteen years old. He was accused of an abduction rape wherein he used a knife and a cigarette lighter to terrorize an eleven-year-old.

Charges were never filed for an undisclosed reason.

Carver brought Trina in for more questioning. He wanted the truth. The truth about who picked her up that night. The truth about Misty.

But the truth was that Trina told the Sgt. Carver and Detective Tom Matison that she lied because she feared "getting into trouble with her guardian about it."

Trina admitted that she called Rhyner, got disconnected and left a message. She told Misty that they could both ride with Rhyner but Misty said no.

"Trina would not be specific why Misty did not trust Rhyner, but the indication was that Rhyner might have 'come on' to Misty at one time and she did not like it. Trina states that she and Rhyner are friends, but not involved."

— Matison's notes

Trina said that she started to walk and then Rhyner picked her up and dropped her off. The detectives asked if perhaps Rhyner had picked up Misty but she said no.

FRANK RODRIGUEZ' FOLLOW UP

Diana would state that Frank Rodriguez, Rheuban's employer, would call her to say that Rheuban had "bragged about doing something" to Misty with his uncle. Frank didn't fully believe him, however, as Rheuban was "weird" and always bragging about stuff he didn't do.

Diana then approached Carver about Rheuban and the sergeant went ballistic.

"We have our man!" he said.

The man he sought was Michael Rhyner, Trina Bevard's boyfriend.

"We share our knowledge of Mike Rhyner and how he is involved with Misty and Trina – and the fact Trina lied to Doyon. We state that there is an excellent possibility that Rhyner may be linked to Chebetnoy and DeLange. Exchange of information is extremely beneficial."

— Carver's notes

"Sgt. Carver believes that Rhyner dropped Bevard off, returned to the area of the fairgrounds, located Misty Copsey, convinced her to get into his vehicle and drove off with her."

— Doyon's notes

Police set up a sting on Rhyner. The car mechanic was selling his 1981 blue Ford Escort for $200 bucks.

The buyer was an undercover cop.

He watched as Rhyner hurriedly took out trash from the car before the sale. The police then did a forensic examination of the car.

Meanwhile, Rheuban's green Nova was being crushed at a wrecking yard. The Puyallup police didn't care as the tweaker was no longer on their radar. Also, Randy Achziger, Bober's suspect, had been charged and convicted for the rape of a seven-year-old.

INTERROGATING RHYNER

Ideally, Detectives Matison and Sgt. Carver wanted the forensics back from Rhyner's Escort before they spoke to him. But the wait became interminable and they brought him in for questioning without some evidence to back up their suspicions.

Rhyner's story would match that of Trina's. He picked Trina up and went back home. He said that he and Trina were only "good friends" and he had met Misty only four times. Matison then asked Rhyner if he felt Misty was alive and what should happen to the person who harmed her.

Rhyner knew what the detective was getting at. On his own volition, Rhyner told the detectives about his juvenile complaint from years ago. He stated he had been cleared and knew that was why they were looking at him now.

"First thing I thought, you know, well, that's in my file," Rhyner said. "Now you guys are going to think I did it since it's in my file. About Misty, that's the one thing that worried me."

Rhyner then passed a polygraph test.

Grasping at straws, the police then turned their sights back on Rheuban. If only they had impounded his car when they had the chance...

TOO LITTLE TOO LATE

"Rheuban Schmidt's initial interview with Sgt. Carver and I created more questions than answers. He was very vague about what he did that September 17th and finally said that he had a 'blackout' and 'woke up' at his grandmother's property near Enumclaw.

...Schmidt had told Frank Rodriguez that Misty's body was six miles from where the jeans were found. He now claims that he said this just to get Rodriguez "off his back," and was not a true statement.

He was driving a Green Chev Nova at the time but he no longer has the vehicle. It was repossessed.

Schmidt also mentioned that his Grandmother's property is located in King County by Buckley and is over a hundred acres. The property has cows on it. Few people enter onto the property."

— Matison's notes

Tinsley, fifteen years old at the time of Misty's disappearance, told police the Rheuban was his roommate for only a few months. He described Rheuban as a short-tempered guy who had a thirteen-year-old girlfriend. The girlfriend, Tinsley said, got jealous when Rheuban got a call from Misty.

Tinsley stated that Rheuban had left the apartment in a huff then came back between eleven and one at night.

So Rheuban did not "black out" as he told detectives. N

"What do you think might have happened to her?" Matison asked.

"Um, I couldn't, I couldn't say because I have no idea," Tinsley said.

"Well, can you speculate?"

"With Rheuban, this is just that I, this, this is what I say with Rheuban because I, I figure that um that he, he tried to, he tried to um, get with her or something and she said, she said no and he got all pissed and did something, I don't know, that's just a second guess."

"You think Rheuban would be capable of ah, kidnapping and killing somebody?"

"I think he could," Tinsley said.

Detectives would meet with Rheuban again, relaying the information that Tinsley recalled him coming back to the apartment that night.

But Rheuban remained adamant in stating that he didn't remember what he did. The detectives then drove him out to his grandmother's farm which had over 100-acres...100 secluded acres.

Detective Matison would note that Rheuban's grandmother's house six miles north of Buckley. Rheuban told Frank that Misty would be buried six miles away from where her jeans were found which would place it in the close vicinity of his grandmother's farm. They would go to inquire with his grandmother but she was not home.

They did not follow-up with the grandmother .

Even so, Rheuban's story no longer held up. He told Misty that he didn't have any gas. He lived sixteen miles away from the fair.

But then he stated that he had driven to his grandmother's farm in Buckley then returned home.

A sixty-mile round trip.

Detectives would give him another polygraph test which he passed.

"It appears that Rheuban Schmidt was not involved in the disappearance of Misty Copsey. He, however, has no alibi as to his movements during the evening of her disappearance, as well as no memory; he claimed that he had a blackout. He acknowledges that he left the residence of James Tinsley, but does not remember what he did.

Investigation to continue."

— Matison's notes

ONE YEAR ANNIVERSARY

The local media ran a few more stories on Misty's disappearance as the Puyallup Fair started. The forensic test on Rhyner's test finally came through. There was no match

with Misty anywhere.

Now once again grasping at straws, Carver would turn to Diana and her associates. He would interview Diana's parole officer and one of her ex-boyfriends.

Misty's father, Buck, was asked to take a polygraph test. He gave consent and passed.

"I explained to her that missing person investigations, at some point in time, must eliminate the parents of any wrongdoing. Diana agreed to the examination."

— Carver's notes

Diana would pass her polygraph test but Jim Corey, Doyon's colleague, said that Diana's polygraph would prove to be inconclusive and that perhaps she had something to do with planting the jeans at the location on Hwy 410.

Carver had always had his doubts about Diana and felt that she planted the jeans.

But the leads would eventually dry up. After nine years, Misty Copsey's disappearance would turn cold.

No one was ever charged with her disappearance.

THE AFTERMATH

Diana would hand out fliers at the Puyallup Fairgrounds every year. She was doing more than law enforcement and even the media.

Every now and then, a local reporter would run a story about Misty. A few cranks would call in and say that they knew something but it would lead to nowhere. Then that would be it. Everything would run dry.

Detective Jim Doyon felt that she was deceased.

BOBER TO THE RESCUE

Bober was then caught for marijuana possession again but this time, he pressed for an advantage. He would gain the Washington State Patrol crime lab report on Misty's jeans, compiled after their 1993 discovery.

He argued that the lab report was part of his defense....he gambled and won.

Obtaining the prized document, the amateur sleuth went to work. The report stated there was no blood, no semen. But there were hairs, fibers, and three red paint chips. There were also holes in the left leg in the jeans, above the knee.

Bober knew that somehow, someway, Randy Achziger was involved. That he killed Misty.

The forensic details raced through Bober's head...red paint chips...red paint chips...

He knew that Bober had a red Porsche. He knew that the paint chips would match.

But the police had another suspect they didn't tell anyone about.

Robert Leslie Hickey.

Hickey's hunting ground was the Puyallup area where he specialized in abduction rapes.

He also drove a red Camaro.

Puyallup police had him on their list as a possible suspect but he was never questioned nor did they obtain forensic samples from his car.

Thirteen years later, however, they would collect samples from Achziger's old car. The car had been sold and the new owner was open to having forensics performed on it.

The particles would be sent to a crime lab which already had a backlog of over a year.

With nothing else left to do, the police turned once again to Rheuban Schmidt.

"I think it's worth taking another shot at Schmidt, and we're planning on it. He's been clean since 1993 ...

— Excerpt from notes by Lt. Dave McDonald, March 19, 2006

Only Schmidt had not been clean. He had been convicted of second-degree theft in 2000. In early 1996, he was accused of rape by one of Misty's best friends. He had held a pillow over her face to silence her but two weeks after filing the report, the girl back away from her accusation and did not file charges.

"[She] told me that she would be undergoing counseling related to the rape, but that she did not want to undergo any additional stress that may be caused by further investigation or possible prosecution in this matter.

Case cleared exceptional/refused by victim."

— Pierce County sheriff's report, Feb. 6, 1996

Later in 2006, Puyallup police gathered more reports on Rheuban. One was a domestic violence protection order requested by his wife, the mother of his three children.

"Rheuban has previously told her that if she ever had him served with a court order he'd 1) burn her house down with her and her kids in it, and 2) send 'some guys' to kick in her door and take money from her.

(She) said Rheuban told her that they'd get money from her if they had to beat her, rape her and then rob her.

(She) said Rheuban told her that if it came to that she 'wouldn't be breathing' when they were done with her."

— Pierce County Sheriff's report, Nov. 9, 2006

MISSING PAINT CHIPS

Adding more incompetence to the investigation, the red paint chips found on Misty's jeans would turn up "missing." All that remained inside the bag where the chips were marked was a piece of plastic.

The lab technicians now had no way to match the red chips on Misty's jeans to Achziger's red Porsche.

Bober would claim that the red chips did match and the police were now trying to save face. Diana, however, no longer wants anything to do with him.

Bober would state that the police would tell Diana that they had, in fact, tested the red paint found on Misty's clothes against Achziger's Porsche. Bober discovered that the red paint was missing beforehand yet the police would lie to Diana about the test.

The lies and incompetence that began investigation have seemingly ended it as well. The Puyallup police relied far too heavily on polygraph tests to discount suspects where their own accounts (particularly in the case of Schmidt) were shaky at best. They failed to secure possession of Schmidt's Green Nova which may have proven to provide forensic evidence that Misty was in his vehicle.

Twenty-four years have elapsed since Misty's disappearance.

Her case remains unsolved.

RAILROAD KILLER

They called him the 'Railroad Killer.'

Angel Resendiz earned the nickname because of his penchant for committing his crimes near railroads, using the rail cars as his own personal get-away system.

Committing murder after murder, he was able to elude both American and Mexican authorities for over a decade.

EARLY LIFE

A birth certificate found by the FBI listed his date of birth as August 1st, 1960. He was born To Virginia de Maturino in the town of Izucar de Matomoros in the state of Puebla, Mexico. His mother has stated adamantly that the correct spelling of his surname is Recendis not Resendiz although the killer would have over fifty different aliases throughout his lifetime.

Angel had spent his childhood years with relatives and not with his immediate family. According to his mother, he was sexually abused by an uncle and other pedophiles in the town of Puebla. He would spend his youth roaming the streets, robbing, stealing and sniffing glue. Relatives would later testify that Resendiz was routinely beaten as a child, one time being "jumped" by several other youths who beat him so bad that he bled through his ears. Resendiz would leave home for months at a time then suddenly return mumbling about a coming religious apocalypse.

Legal trouble came early for Resendiz as he was caught trying to sneak into the Texas border at the age of sixteen. This would become the first of numerous run-ins with border patrol agents until he finally made it into the United States, making his way to St. Louis and finding work with a manufacturing company under an assumed name. He even registered to vote with his false identification.

In September of 1979, at the age of nineteen, Resendiz was arrested for assault and car theft in Miami. He was tried and sentenced to twenty-years in prison but was released after only six years and sent back to Mexico.

But he wouldn't stay there for long.

Through numerous attempts of trial and error, Resendiz had learned not only to game the system but to enter and exit the United States with minimal detection.

He learn to use the rail-cars...

AN "INVISIBLE" MAN

Resendiz became so skilled at crossing the border without detection that he began charging for his services. He began to make a living as a human smuggler, transporting Mexicans across the border for a fee.

Resendiz soon developed a reputation for his smuggling skills, often being seen as a 'go to' person in his Ciudad Juarez neighborhood called 'Patria.'

He would make weekly crossings over the border, being arrested only intermittently. He would then be deported back into his native land only to ping-pong back and forth.

Finally, Resendiz would serve prison terms for his crimes. He would be arrested in Texas for false identity and citizenship, getting a year and half worth of jail.

Upon release in 1987, he journeyed to New Orleans and was arrested for carrying a concealed weapon. He received another year and half worth of prison time until parole.

He then went back to his old haunts in St. Louis where he tried to defraud Social Security and receive illegal payments. He got caught and served a three year sentence.

Resendiz then decided small-time burglaries were his deal. He once again illegally crossed the border, journeyed to New Mexico and was caught burglarizing a home. He was imprisoned for eighteen months and upon release he broke into a Santa Fe rail yard, being captured yet again.

"They should have called Resendiz the boomerang man," forensic psychologist Frank Lizzo said. "He knew how to play the game and seemingly had no fear of the system. The system never punished him severely enough for him to stop his crimes, let alone stop crossing the border."

After his last recorded deportation, the killings began.

THE KILLING FIELDS

"He probably started killing somewhere in his late 20s," Douglas said. "He may have killed people like himself initially – males, transients...(he) became angry at the population at large. What America represents here is this wealthy country where he keeps getting kicked out...(he) just can't make ends meet. Coupled with these feelings, these inadequacies, fueled by the fact that he's known to take alcohol, take drugs, lowers his inhibitions now to go out and kill."

Angel's list of victims began in 1986. Continuing to bounce in and out of the United States, he shot a homeless woman and left her for dead in an abandoned farm house. He had met the acquaintance of the woman at a homeless shelter and they became friends. They would later take a trip on a motorcycle together when he felt that the woman disrespected him.

Resendiz would then take out his gun and blow her head off.

The woman allegedly had a boyfriend whom Resendiz shot and killed as well. He said that he dumped his body in a creek between San Antonio and Uvalde. This killing has never been verified aside from what Resendiz revealed to the police during his interrogation sessions.

Five years later, Resendiz would kill Michael White because he was a "homosexual." Resendiz would bludgeon White to death with a brick and leave him in front of an abandoned home.

These were seemingly warm-ups for the more brutal crimes to come which would also include rape.

"Sex seemed almost secondary," FBI profiler John Douglas said when apprised of Resendiz's crimes. "(He is) just a bungling crook ...very disorganized."

Douglas would later concede, however, that it was this disorganization that worked in his favor. Like a true drifter, Resendiz' whereabouts became as elusive as a rational thought in his head.

"When he hitches a ride on the freight train, he doesn't necessarily know where the train is going," Douglas said. "But when he gets off, having background as a burglar, he's able to scope out the area, do a little surveillance, make sure he breaks into the right house where there won't be anyone to give him a run for his money. He can enter a home complete with cutting glass and reaching in and undoing the locks."

"He'll look through the windows and see who's occupying it. The guy's only 5 foot-7, very small. In fact...the early weapons were primarily blunt-force trauma weapons, weapons of opportunity found at the scenes. He has to case them out, make sure he can put himself in a win-win situation."

Resendiz would also leave his weapon of choice up to chance. Whatever the home would have, a statue a mantle piece, a butcher knife, that would become the instrument of murder.

FLORIDA KILLINGS

On March 23rd, 1997, Jesse Howell would be found bludgeoned to death beside the railroad tracks in Ocala, Florida. He was nineteen years old.

"When we got there," Sheriff Patty Lumpkin said. "We see what appears to be a young male, in his late teens or early twenties. Blood around the head area. You could tell by looking at him that he was dead. The first thing I do is make sure that we've got our forensics people on the way, on the medical examiners on the way, and all the investigators that we have called out or either there or en route."

"When those types of things happen it might have been someone who had fallen off a train," Lt. Jeff Owens said. "Or someone who could have been struck by a train."

The authorities quickly ruled out an accident, however, as they examined the body.

"It didn't appear to be an accident," Lumpkin said. "Because if he had been hit by the train the trauma would have been much more extreme. I've seen some deaths from trains and the initial impact from the train would have done more harm to the body."

The forensic team did determine that Howell's body looked as if he were the victim of blunt force trauma.

"We did see a baseball type of cap," forensic scientist Michael Dunn said. "It appeared to have blood on the inside surface of he bill. In addition, there was a pair of wire rimmed eye glasses and one of the eye pieces was missing, one of the lenses was out. This didn't look good either. As we moved closer, we saw that the victim had been dragged to that spot using just the blue jean material around the cuff (of his pants)."

Near the body, they found a brass and rubber coupling. This device was used to link one train car to another. It could also be used as a clubbing weapon.

"It had what appeared to be blood on it (the coupling)," Dunn recalled.

Howell still had jewelry on his person. He wore a gold cross necklace, a watch and a small amount of cash in his pocket. The police ruled out robbery as a motive.

The police did not identify Howell's body right off the bat. They did find a money wire receipt where some money had been wired from Illinois to Florida. The name on the receipt was of a woman named "Wendy."

Police tracked the money transfer to its point of origin which was all the way in Woodstock, Illinois.

Coincidentally, the authorities there were investigating the disappearance of Wendy Von Huben.

Wendy was missing alongside her boyfriend, the nineteen year old Jesse Howell.

"They advised me that they were investigating a John Doe," Woodstock Detective Kurt Rosenquest recalled. "Unidentified male."

Rosenquest then followed up with the investigating team in Florida, sending them the fingerprints and pictures of Jesse Howell.

The Ocala police would then positively identify Howell.

Jesse had met Wendy only months earlier. They had secretly planned to marry and went on a road trip with another couple.

The other couple, however, grew tired of Jesse and Wendy's constant bickering. They demanded to be let out of the car and left. Jesse and Wendy continued into Ocala, Florida where they ran out of money.

Wendy would call her parents in Illinois who would then transfer her $200 via Western Union. The couple would collect the $200 but would not return home.

"We checked Greyhounds," Rosenquest said. "Nobody matching their description ordered buses or train tickets back to the Woodstock area."

Tears were shed as Rosenquest informed Howell's parents that their teen son had been murdered. The investigative team then turned their attention to the disappearance of Wendy.

They held out hope because there were issues between her and Jesse, thinking that perhaps she simply ran off to be by herself.

Police scoured the surrounding areas and used helicopters in all directions around the railroad tracks.

They would find nothing. There was no DNA left behind on Jesse Howell's body either.

Papers and fliers with Wendy Von Huben's information was distributed all throughout Florida up through Illinois.

Authorities also began interviewing the transient population that lived along the railroad tracks.

Two and a half months later, however, Wendy's parents would receive a phone call.

"The phone rang," Rosenquest recalled. "Wendy's father answered the phone. The girl was crying. She said 'I'm sorry. I love you.'"

She would tell the father she was two hours away from Woodstock at a gas station. The father asked for the phone number on the pay phone she was calling from and she said that there wasn't any before hanging up.

The police were not certain that the phone call came from Wendy so they immediately headed out to the gas station where they believe the call took place.

Police tracked down the surveillance video of the gas station. On the video, a woman that physically resembled Wendy entered the gas station.

The phone records, however, revealed that the call did not come from the gas station where the surveillance video revealed a woman who allegedly was Wendy. It came from another gas station where there were fliers posted of Wendy.

Someone had played a cruel hoax as Wendy's parents had added their home number to the fliers

ONE-LEGGED BOB AND A CHANCE DISCOVERY

A year went by without any sign of Wendy.

There was some ray of hope, however, as the railroad authorities called the Ocala police and informed them that the received information from a member of one of the homeless camps. They had a man in custody named "One Legged Bob" who was traveling with a girl and may be responsible for the murder of her previous boyfriend.

"'One Legged Bob' was your typical homeless person," Owens said. "Kinda scruffy. Hadn't shaved in a few days. He had a prosthetic leg that helped him get around. For someone who you might consider crippled, he was far from crippled."

Owens would spend the next eight hours interviewing the only lead he had, a one legged homeless man.

After the grueling interrogation, Owens realized that he had the wrong suspect.

By sheer chance, however, Patty Lumpkin heard about someone they dubbed the "Railroad Killer" during a class she was taking at the FBI.

"They called him the Railway Killer," Lumpkin recalled. "The Angel of Death. He was killing people. Leaving them near the railroad or he was killing them at homes or locations that were close to the railroad.

The FBI knew the Railway Killer as Angel Resendiz.

"We knew that Angel Resendiz was a person that rode the rails across the country," FBI Agent Mark Young said. "We were worried where he'd wind up next. So we decided to make him a top ten fugitive. Maybe the millions of eyes of the public would tell us something."

The strategy worked.

"He was one of the most vile, evil persons that I had ever dealt with," Young said. "It was like every time you turn around there's another murder."

Owens and Lumpkin hoped to talk to Resendiz to query him about Jesse Howell's murder and Wendy Von Huben's disappearance.

"The attorneys representing him at the time in Texas stopped us," Owens said. "They wanted to protect their client from talking. Any defense attorney who represents a criminal will generally tell the person to stop talking to law enforcement."

Resendiz was placed on death row and Texas had a fast execution rate. The two detectives worried that they would lose their chance to interview Resendiz and connect him to the crimes in Ocala.

Owens and Lumpkin decided to mail Resendiz a letter, respectfully asking him if they could interview him. The letter was written in a formal manner and even addressed him as "Senor."

To their surprise, Resendiz responded back and granted them an interview regarding his involvement in Jesse's killing and Wendy's disappearance.

During their meeting, Resendiz was quick to admit that he had killed Jesse. The detectives deliberately withheld information about the killing, holding back details that only the killer would know. But when Resendiz described using a brake coupling from one of the trains, they knew they had their killer.

But they needed to find out what happened to Wendy.

In a follow-up letter, they promised him immunity from prosecution if he agreed to talk. It was a moot point by then as he was already on death row but the detectives still needed permission from Wendy's family to go through with the interview.

In order to receive some sense of closure, the family agreed to the immunity.

"When we get to the prison," Lumpkin said. "We see him coming down the hallway. He (Resendiz) has a waist belt on. It's an electric shock belt and he's chained to the belt. He's just a mild-mannered person but remember that a psychopath or a sociopath doesn't have any feeling. I mean he had dead eyes. He had no feeling in that body. He didn't care about anything."

Resendiz would reveal that he was heading south for work when the train stopped and he spotted Jesse getting off the train for a smoke.

"Resendiz told us that he killed Jesse with a piece of the train coupling," Lumpkin said. "And Wendy was asleep on the train when this took place. And then when they went down the road further somehow he talked Wendy into getting off the train."

Resendiz then raped and strangled Wendy to death.

Resendiz drew a map of where had left Wendy's body. He described burying her in a shallow grave near a canopy of trees. Resendiz would remember that she had a book in a back pack and an army style jacket that he used to cover her fresh grave.

Police would return to the site and were able to locate where he buried Wendy's body. Almost three years after the murder, everything the killer described was still there. The book. The jacket.

And Wendy's body.

"When Wendy ran away she had a small engagement ring," Owen said. "And she had a Winnie the Pooh wristwatch.

The detective would bring those items back to Wendy's parents.

KENTUCKY RAILROAD MURDER

In August of 1997, Resendiz would make his way from Ocala, Florida to Lexington, Kentucky. It was there he would stalk two young college students.

Holly Dunn was a 20-year old junior at the University of Kentucky and it was there she met Christopher Maier.

"Chris Maier was my very good friend," Dunn recalled. "He was just the nicest, kindest man. We decided that we wanted to be more than friends then we started dating. We dated for about three months."

"Chris and I were attending a party. We decided that the party wasn't very fun so we went to go talk a walk by the railroad tracks. We sat down and talked for awhile and when we got up to leave a man came out from behind an electrical box. He had a weapon that he used on Chris. It was some sort of ice pick or screw driver. Something sharp. I guess our immediate thought was he's going to rob us. That's when we realize he wants money we start thinking 'okay, well, you could have our credit card, you can have our ATM card, you can have our car.' Then he started tying up Chris' hands behind his back. And then he came over to me and he took off my belt and that's when I started thinking he doesn't want to rob us."

After tying up Holly, Resendiz then pulled Chris by the shirt across the railroad tracks and into a ditch.

Holly would follow on her knees, pleading for him to stop whatever he was about to do.

"Lie down," Resendiz said, his voice soft but menacing.

"Everything is going to be okay," Christopher said to Holly as Resendiz dragged him into the ditch.

"Shut up!" Resendiz commanded as he gagged Christopher with a sock.

Resendiz then walked off into the darkness. The frightened couple did not know what the psychopath had planned.

"Then he comes with this rock," Holly recalled. "There was no warning, he drops this rock on Chris' head. I'm just thinking 'what just happened?' I don't even know what just happened."

"You don't have to worry about him anymore," Resendiz said to Holly as he got on top of her.

"I went into survival mode, I'm thinking, I mean he's gonna kill me. I may as well fight. I'm gonna fight. He unties my feet and climbs on top of me. I start to kick and scream and hit him but he held that knife or ice pick (to my throat) and said 'look how easily I could kill you.' I stopped everything and then he raped me."

"I memorized his face," Dunn said. "I stared at him and memorized, he had a tattoo on his arm, I was thinking if you have any scars I'm gonna remember your scars, I'm gonna remember your face,I'm not gonna forget it because if I live through this I will get you."

Resendiz completed the sexual assault of Dunn before smashing her head with a rock.

"He hit me five or six times in my face," Dunn recalled. "I think I put my hand up and then I turned over and then he hit me five or six times in the back of my head. He hit me hard. He was trying to kill me. I think I laid there and he thought I was dead."

Resendiz did think she was did as he threw the rock down and ran away from the crime scene.

Holly would suffer severe facial trauma but miraculously survived the attack.

"I had a broken jaw," Dunn said. "Broken eye socket and cuts on the back of my head that they had to staple shut and then I had cuts on my face."

She woke up in a Kentucky hospital, surrounded by family members.

"Everyone was told not to talk about Chris to me. I just said 'Chris is dead, isn't he?' And my Dad actually is the one I said that to and he was like 'yes, he died.'"

TEXAS TERROR

Resendiz would travel to Texas via train and in October of 1988 he flopped down in Hughes Springs. He would enter the home of 87-year old Leafie Mason, attacking the woman with an iron and killing her.

Two months later, Resendiz would sneak into the home of Dr. Claudia Benton, a thirty-nine year old medical researcher who lived in a suburb of Houston near the railroad tracks.

Again, it was a case of a home being to close to the train tracks. The train would provide the perfect cover for the sneaky Resendiz as he realized that the sound of the rail-car racing by would allow him to break in homes without being heard.

He applied the same technique with Benton, breaking into her home, raping then killing her.

Police would find the doctor face down on the floor. Her bedroom soaked in blood, ransacked for any valuables.

He head had been covered in a plastic bag while her body had been covered in a blanket.

"It appears that she (Claudia Benton) was sleeping," recalled Ken Macha, former police sergeant. "He was able to get in and picked up a bronze statuette from the mantle in the living room. He was relentless in beating her. The skull fractures themselves would have been enough to kill her. She was then stabbed in the back with a very large butcher knife."

"Resendiz was brutal, sadistic," said former West University police chief Gary Brye.

Fingerprints and DNA evidence would link Resendiz to the crime.

The problem was they could catch the man that Texas Ranger Drew Carter referred to as "a walking, breathing form of evil."

EVADING POLICE

Seven months later, Resendiz would continue to avoid capture. He remained in Texas, riding the rail cars until coming into the town of Weimar. He would break into the home of Pastor Norman "Skip" Sirnic and his wife Karen. Resendiz smashed a jack hammer into both of their heads, killing them instantly. He would then rape the body of Karen postmortem.

"He would watch these places," prosecuting attorney Devin Anderson said. "He would watch them, wait for them to go to sleep, get in their house and he would strike them before they would even wake up. I thought we have got to catch this guy."

The DNA found at the scene of the Sirnic murders would match those left on Benton. The FBI then realized they had a highly mobile serial killer on the loose...someone who could kill in one town then appear in another town miles away and kill again.

Resendiz was also smart. He would constantly alter his appearance. He'd shave his head. Then his mustache. He'd be clean shaven one week. Unkempt the next. He would wear glasses one week. No glasses the next.

Authorities could not get an accurate description of him other than the fact that he was small.

Resendiz was also able to take advantage of the lack of a coordinated computer system that gave law enforcement the ability to cross-check fugitives. After the Sirnic murders, Border Patrol had encountered Resendiz near the El Paso border but did not find him on the wanted list.

They then deported him back to Mexico.

Within 48 hours, Resendiz was back across the border to resume his killing spree.

"Our computers told us that he was nothing of lookout material," said C.G. Almengor, a supervisor at the border."We really wish he had been in the system so we could have caught him."

Resendiz would be deported no less than seventeen times over the course of his rampage. At no point did authorities make the connection because of his changing appearance, use of different aliases and the lack of a connected system to document illegals trying to come across the border.

A PREFERENCE FOR TEXAS

Noemi Dominguez was a graduate of Rice University who had just recently quit her job as an elementary school teacher to pursue a master's degree.

She was described as "the sweetest, nicest teacher – a darling who went the extra mile."

Fueled by hate, Resendiz would break into Noemi's home and rape her before killing her with a pick ax. He then stole her car and drove to Schulenberg, Texas where he would kill Josephine Konvicka with the same pick ax.

He would leave the weapon embedded in Konvicka's head as well as leave his fingerprints all over the home. He was more than just sloppy, he was getting cocky. He left a newspaper article that described his crimes as well as a toy train...a reference to his nickname as the "Railroad Killer."

Resendiz was also meticulous in approaching his victims.

"He undid the light in her (Noemi's) car," Anderson said. "So when he opened the door it wouldn't come on. That's who were were dealing with. Someone who really knew how to sneak around. Who really knew how to avoid detection."

"He kept killing people. He would not stop. In his mode of transportation, using the railroads was brilliant because they couldn't be monitored. I mean there's thousands of trains and millions of miles of tracks all over the United States."

"I felt hopeless at the time. Because if you're willing to sleep in a train or you're willing to sleep in a field, you can stay lost for a long, long time and I didn't think we were ever going to catch him."

Later that month, Resendiz had journeyed to Illinois, reaching the town of Gorham. He would break into the home of 80-year old George Morber and his daughter Carolyn Frederick. Resendiz would tie Morber to a chair and shoot him in the back of the head with a shotgun. He then raped Carolyn and smashed the shotgun across her head with such force that the weapon broke in half.

Both Morber and Frederick would die from their injuries.

The FBI placed him on their Top Ten list.

They then recruited his common-law wife, Julietta Reyes, and brought her into Houston for questioning from her hometown of Rodeo, Mexico.

Reyes complied with police requests, turning over over ninety-three pieces of jewelry that her husband had mailed to her from the U.S.

Relatives of Noemi Dominguez claimed thirteen pieces. George Benton was able to identify some pieces of jewelry as belonging to his wife as well.

Police would then locate Resendiz's half-sister, Manuela Karkiewicz, who lived in New Mexico. Initially, she refused to cooperate. She worried that the FBI or the police would kill her brother. But Carter convinced her to talk Resendiz into giving himself up.

The FBI knew that Resendiz had made his way back to Mexico after the murders in Illinois and was hiding in his hometown neighborhood of Patria.

Carter was able to get a rapport with Manuela. He convinced her that Resendiz would receive "personal safety while in jail, regular visiting rights for his family and a psychological evaluation."

"I came away with the impression that they (Resendiz' family) definitely had an understanding of right and wrong ... and knew now that what Maturino Resendiz was accused of doing was heinous and wrong ... ," Carter said. "Manuela, especially, came across as a woman of strong faith. There was a very deep emotional strain and burden placed on her in this investigation. She had to make some very difficult choices that impacted her and her family. And, in the end, her actions alone speak to her character."

Carter spent weeks talking to Manuela who in turn "worked a miracle."

They got the serial killer to surrender.

On July 12th, Manuela would receive a fax from the district attorney's office in Harris County which formalized everything that Texas Ranger Carter had promised.

The word passed from Manuela to another relative who acted as a go-between with Resendiz. The relative than came back later that evening and said that Resendiz would surrender in the morning at 9 a.m.

Texas Ranger Drew Carter would accompany Manuela and a spiritual adviser to meet with Resendiz on a bridge that connected El Paso, Texas to Ciudad Juarez.

"When I saw that face there was a little bit of excitement there because I finally said, 'This is going to happen,'" Carter recalled as he remembered Resendiz appearing on the bridge with his dirty jeans, muddy boots and blank facial expression. "He stuck out his hand, I stuck out my hand, and we shook hands."

Resendiz would then surrender to the Texas Ranger.

DEATH PENALTY

Resendiz' attorneys knew that their only hope would be an insanity defense. The Mexican government also got involved, lobbying authorities to spare Resendiz the death penalty

"Insanity was the logical defense because no one wants to believe that there is someone out there who would do things like that," Anderson said. "That was the thing that worried me the most about the case was that jurors would just throw up their hands and say nobody in their right mind could do what he does."

"The thing about what a life sentence with Resendiz would have been, he would have enjoyed it. I mean he would have had pen pals. He would have given interviews if they let him, I mean he would have loved it. And I knew that. And he didn't deserve to live after what he did just didn't. He caused so much pain, so much heartache and so much terror, that's what the whole focus of the trial had to be."

George Benton, the husband of Claudia, would vehemently criticize the Mexican government who support his appeals and domestic opposition to the death penalty.

"(He)looked like a man and walked like a man. But what lived within that skin was not a human being."

"He was small," Anderson said when she first saw Resendiz in the courtroom. "Maybe five- foot five. His forearms though, were roped with muscles. He was scary. Even though he was small you could feel he was dangerous. He looked like a wild animal who'd been caught."

Resendiz looked "timid" in the courtroom and spoke of himself in religious riddles. He claimed he was Jewish and didn't seem effected when he was informed that the prosecution was aiming for the death penalty.

"I don't believe in death," Resendiz, said. "I know the body is going to go to waste. But me, as a person, I'm eternal. I'm going to be alive forever."

The defense said that Resendiz' crimes were caused by head injuries, drug abuse and a family history of mental illness. He has a delusional perception of the world as he believes that he can cause earthquakes, floods, and explosions and that God told him to kill his victims whom they believed to be evil.

He made a living stealing things from his victims and having his wife sell them in Mexico. "That was his job," Anderson said. "And for recreation it was killing the people who lived in the house."

"He was a very intelligent person who worked the system and knew exactly what kinds of things to say to get that defense to work."

The jury, however, would find Resendiz guilty after one hour and forty-five minutes of deliberation.

He was sentenced to die via lethal injection.

"He made it very clear during my conversation with him that he deserves to die," Owens said.

"I want to ask if it is in your heart to forgive me," Resendiz said in his final words. "You don't have to. I know I allowed the devil to rule my life. I just ask you to forgive me and ask the Lord to forgive me for allowing the devil to deceive me. I thank God for having patience with me. I don't deserve to cause you pain. You did not deserve this. I deserve what I am getting."

Resendiz then prayed in Hebrew and Spanish before drawing his final breath.

MISSING MADELEINE

MARY CHILDRESS

Madeleine McCann, a young child of three years old, was visiting the popular Portuguese resort town of Praia da Luiz along with her parents and younger siblings, as well as a group of her parents' close friends, when she went missing on the night of May 3rd. Madeleine's disappearance became an international sensation and various police departments in both Portugal and the United Kingdom, as well as Madeleine's parents, would conduct independent investigations into her disappearance and the circumstances surrounding that night.

Background

Madeleine Beth McCann was born on May 12th, 2003 to Gerry and Kate McCann in the small town of Leicester, in the United Kingdom, before moving to Rothley in Leicestershire as a young child. Both Gerry and Kate McCann were both practicing physicians and prominent members of the local Roman Catholic community, and had a total of three young children at the time of Madeleine's disappearance, Madeleine as well as two younger siblings: a twin boy and girl.

The entire McCann family set out for the popular Portuguese resort town of Praia da Luz (referred to as "little Britain" because of the large amount of British vacationers who frequented the town) on Saturday, April 28th for a family vacation with seven other adults and five additional children.

The McCanns rented a small apartment owned by a retired British schoolteacher through a private vacation company. The unit, a two-bedroom ground level apartment in the resort's Waterside Village, was next door to several of their friends' rented apartments. The unit was accessible from two locations: a sliding glass patio door and a front door facing the popular Ocean Club. The room's sliding glass door and patio overlooked the Ocean Club's facilities, including the tapas bar that Madeleine's parents would dine at the night of her disappearance.

The nine adults who made up the party included the McCann parents, Russell O'Brien, Matthew Oldfield and his spouse, Rachael

Oldfield, Dianne Webster, David Payne, Fiona Payne, and Jane Tanner and her significant other. These friends would later be referred to as the "Tapas Seven," after the tapas bar that they were dining at the night of Madeleine's disappearance.

Night of Disappearance

During the daytime on May 3rd, the group's last night at the resort, the children spent the morning playing at the resort's Kids' Club, also eating lunch with their parents and spending a couple of hours at the children's pool. The last known photo of Madeleine was taken that afternoon by Kate McCann, showing the young girl sitting by the pool next to her father and sister.

On the night of Madeleine's disappearance, her mother put Madeleine and her siblings down for bed around 7:00pm, wearing her favorite Marks and Spencer's Eeyore pajamas. At 8:30pm, the group of nine adults decided to have dinner and drinks at the nearby tapas bar, located just 160 feet away from the hotel rooms that the children were staying in. Kate McCann described the tapas bar as being located directly across the pool from the children's room and being just a 30-second walk away.

The group of adults had requested a table on the patio which overlooked their children's rooms, so that the parents could have peace of mind while dining. Kate McCann has stated that a resort staff member left a note in the message book in the swimming pool area stating that the group of adults was requesting a specific table so that they would have a view of the hotel rooms in which their children were staying in. She has indicated that she believes the kidnapper saw this note earlier in the day and decided to kidnap her Madeleine upon realizing that the children were to be left unguarded at night.

The McCanns stated that the group of adults agreed to check on the children every 30 minutes, with each adult taking a different shift and helping to check on the eight children located in several different rooms. Because the McCann's patio doors could only be unlocked from the inside, the McCanns left the curtain down and doors closed, but left the patio door unlocked. This is presumably how the kidnapper was able to enter the room. It should be noted that the parents also set up a child-safety gate at both the top of the patio stairs and at the bottom, making it extremely unlikely that Madeleine wandered out of the room.

Gerry McCann performed the first check on his children at 9:05pm, and he reported the children as sleeping safely and soundly. However, he did notice that the children's bedroom door, which he had left open just an inch or two, was nearly wide open when he performed his check on the children. This was the last time that either of the parents would see Madeleine.

Matthew Oldfield, a friend of the McCanns and member of the Tapas Seven, volunteers to check on all of the children at 9:30pm (his children were sleeping in the room next door). When he enters the McCann's room, he notices that the children's bedroom door was wide open. However, he states that upon hearing no noises, he left the apartment without physically looking inside of the children's room. He later states that he did not notice whether there was a draft or whether the bedroom window was open. The fact that he volunteered to check on the children and his claim that he did not actually look in the room caused him to be viewed as a primary suspect by the local police department.

Roughly thirty minutes later, at 10:00pm, Kate McCann walks back to her hotel room to check on her children. Kate stated that she entered the apartment through the patio door and immediately noticed that the children's bedroom door was completely open. Noticing nothing amiss and hearing no noises, Kate attempted to close the bedroom door without looking inside. However, the door closed rapidly and loudly, as if there was a strong draft pulling the door closed.

When Kate reopened the door to see where the draft was coming from, she noticed that the children's window and shutter were both open and that Madeleine was missing from her bed. The young girl's blanket and favorite stuffed toy were still lying on the bed, but her daughter was nowhere to be seen. After frantically searching the apartment for Madeleine, Kate began running back towards the restaurant screaming that her daughter had been taken.

Upon hearing from Kate, Gerry McCann asked Matthew Oldfield to go to the hotel lobby and contact the police. The hotel staff called the local police department at 10:30am and began mobilizing their staff and willing guests to help in the search for young Madeleine. The combined 60 hotel staff members and guests searched for Madeleine until 4:30am, screaming her name throughout the resort.

Police Arrival

At approximately 11:10pm, two officers from the national military police arrive to investigate the missing child report. After conducting a brief search of the resort, they contact the local police force to assist with the search. Two officers from the local police force arrive at 11:20pm to begin assisting with the search and to investigate the hotel room. Later that morning, both patrol dogs and search and rescue dogs were brought in to assist with the search for Madeleine. A road block was not put into place until 10:00am that morning.

The initial police response consisted of a variety of mistakes and oversights that prevented crucial evidence from being gathered. First of all, more than twenty different people were allowed to enter the apartment before it was closed off for investigation, potentially corrupting a wide range of evidence. In addition, although police officers did place "Do Not Enter" crime scene tape over the doorway to the children's room at 3:00am, they did not secure the apartment itself from people entering it. In addition, although police did not allow tourists to stay in the apartment for a full month after Madeleine's disappearance, tourists were again allowed to stay in the apartment for several months until it was closed off to the public again in August 2007 for additional forensic testing and analysis.

Police officers also allowed a fairly substantial crowd of people to congregate on the patio, directly outside of the children's window. It is thought that a great deal of forensic evidence was corrupted as a result of this. Additionally, the officer responsible for dusting the children's window and gathering fingerprint evidence did so without using gloves, possibly corrupting yet another set of evidence.

Furthermore, during the manhunt for Madeleine, several additional mistakes were made. The police did not provide a description of Madeleine or pictures of the young girl to the border police or coast guard force until several hours after her disappearance. Roadblocks were also not put into place until 10:00am that morning, meaning that Madeleine could have been in another country by the time key law enforcement figures even began to search for her. Lastly, Interpol, the global anti-crime organization, did not issue an alert about her disappearance for a full five days after she was reported as missing, allowing her kidnappers crucial time to escape and transport her out of the country or even out of the continent.

Child Sightings

Jane Tanner

Jane Tanner, one of the "Tapas Seven," reported seeing a man carrying a child through the resort complex the night of the disappearance. Jane left the tapas bar at 9:00pm to personally check on her own children in their nearby hotel room and reported passing Madeleine's father, on his way back from checking on his own children, during her walk to the hotel room.

While Jane claimed to have seen Gerry McCann on her way to check on her own children, both Gerry and an English vacationer that he stopped to chat with, do not remember seeing her pass by on the very narrow street. This discrepancy later cast doubt on her story and led to Portuguese authorities accusing her of inventing the story.

At approximately 9:10pm, Jane reported that she saw a man and a child cross the street at *Rua Dr Francisco Gentil Martins* and *Rua Dr Agostinho da Silva* heading away from the Ocean Club, towards the east. She described the man looking like a local and as carrying a barefoot child across the intersection. The man was described as being of Mediterranean appearance, dark-haired, roughly 5' 7" tall, and wearing khakis with a dark jacket. The child was seen wearing light-colored pink pajamas with floral patterns. Although Jane reported this sighting to the local police department soon after Madeleine was discovered missing, the police did not release any information on this possible suspect until some three weeks later, on May 25th.

Despite Jane's seemingly important sighting, a later investigation by Scotland Yard would rule out this individual as a suspect. British police were able to identify the man as a vacationer staying in the same resort as the McCanns. He was carrying his daughter back to their hotel room after picking her up from a play hour for children at the resort. It would later be confirmed that his daughter was wearing light-pink pajamas with floral prints that night.

Martin and Mary Smith

Two other vacationers staying at the resort reporting seeing a man carrying a young child the night of Madeleine's disappearance. Martin and Mary Smith reported seeing a man walking down Rua da Escola Primaria, towards Rua 25 de Abril and away from the resort, at approximately 10:00pm that night. The man was sighted just 500 yards from the McCann's apartment.

The Smiths stated that the man did not look like a tourist and that he did not seem comfortable interacting with the child in his arms. The man was described as being in his mid-30s, approximately 5' 8", with short brown hair and khakis on. The child was described as being three or four years old, with blond hair and light colored pajamas. The young girl was also barefoot.

Those Present at Time of Disappearance

The McCanns were accompanied by a group of seven adults and five children on their vacation to Praia da Luz. All seven adults were present at the tapas bar for at least part of the night. Jane Tanner, an English marketing executive, and her partner Russell O'Brien were staying in one room with their two children. Fiona and David Payne, as well as Fiona's mother, Dianne Webster, and their two children were staying in another room. Lastly, Matthew Oldfield and his wife, Rachael Oldfield, were staying in the last room along with their young daughter.

Timeline

7:00pm - Gerry and Kate McCann put their three children to bed. The children are all sleeping in the bedroom closest to the front door.

8:30pm - Gerry and Kate McCann leave the hotel to meet their friends at the resort's tapas bar, located just 160 feet from the hotel room and in sight of the patio door. The parents reportedly leave the patio door unlocked, but the door closed and the curtains drawn.

9:05pm - Gerry McCann checks on the children in their room. He reports that the children were sleeping safe and sound. He stops to speak with another tourist for a few minutes on his was back to the tapas bar.

9:10pm - Jane Tanner recalls seeing Gerry speaking with the English tourist on the street leading back to the tapas bar. Neither man recalls seeing Jane Tanner, which casts doubt on her story given how narrow the street was. Tanner notices a man crossing the street with a child in his arms. This sighting is later ruled out by Scotland Yard detectives.

9:30pm - Matthew Oldfield, a member of the Tapas Seven, visits the McCann's room to check on the children. He notices that the bedroom door is wide open, but upon hearing no noise, he does not go far enough into the apartment to see whether Madeleine is in bed. He does not recall the bedroom window being open at this time.

10:00pm - Martin and Mary Smith, two tourists staying in the same resort, recall seeing a man carrying a barefoot child down the street, away from the resort.

10:00pm - Kate McCann visits the hotel room to check on her children. She entered the apartment through the patio doors and noticed that the bedroom door was wide open and then sees that the window is open as well. She notices that Madeleine is missing and, after performing a quick check of the entire apartment, runs back to the restaurant screaming that her daughter is missing.

10:10pm - Gerry McCann asks the resort to call the police and report Madeleine as missing.

10:30pm - The hotel begins treating Madeleine's disappearance as a missing childrens case. The hotel mobilizes sixty staff members and guests to search the entire resort complex for Madeleine. Reportedly, guests could hear Madeleine's name being screamed out until 4:30am that morning.

11:10pm - Two officers from the Guarda Nacional Republicana, essentially the country's military police, arrive at the resort to conduct a search for Madeleine. After conducting a quick search, they contact the local criminal police department for assistance.

11:20pm - Two officers from the Policia Judiciaria, the local police department, arrive to assist with the search and investigate the McCann's hotel room for clues.

2:00am - Two patrol dogs arrive at the resort to assist with the search for Madeleine.

8:00am - Four search and rescue dogs arrive at the resort to search for Madeleine. Local police officers are called in from vacation and during their days off to assist with the search. They begin searching local waterways, wells, and sewers.

10:00am - Police setup road blocks to prevent the abductor from leaving with the child. The local police department did not ask for photos of cars seen leaving the area at the time of Madeleine's disappearance.

Portuguese Investigation

Portuguese investigators interviewed several witnesses who reported seeing a group of two strange men in the area of the McCann's apartment the morning of the abduction, as well as several days earlier. On the day of Madeleine's disappearance, two men were spotted visiting the area surrounding the McCann's apartment, with one man being spotted on the actual street. The two men, who were visiting the area from 3:30 to 5:30pm the evening of Madeleine's disappearance, said that they were visiting tourist rooms in order to collect donations for a local orphanage. Investigators from Scotland Yard would later say that they believed the two men were casing the street and planning their abduction.

Witnesses would also report seeing several blond-haired men around the McCann's apartment in the days leading up to Madeleine's disappearance. Earlier in the day on May 3rd, a man was seen walking through a gate near their apartment, attempting to close the gate door quietly and without being noticed. Later that evening, at least one blond man was seen standing near the McCann's room at 4:00pm and again at 6:00pm.

At 11:00pm that night, two blond men were seen speaking to each other in loud voices, but reportedly lowered their voices and hurried off upon noticing that they were being observed. Witnesses also reported seeing a man leaning against a wall next to the McCann's apartment the day before the disappearance, with a white unmarked van parked next to the apartment. All in all, several witnesses report seeing suspicious men near the McCann's apartment in the days leading up to Madeleine's disappearance, and report seeing the men staring at or watching the McCann's apartment.

Parents' Reaction

In May 2007, Gerry and Kate McCann set up a private fund to investigate the disappearance of their daughter, calling the organization *Madeleine's Fund: Leaving No Stone Unturned.* Over $2.6 million was raised to help in the search for their daughter, and the British publication *News of the World* offered a $1.5 million reward for information leading to her return or conclusively proving her fate. Despite the creation of the fund, the McCanns were accused of using the money to pay for their mortgage payment on at least two occasions. The fund has yet to make any progress on ascertaining the fate of Madeleine McCann.

Scotland Yard Investigation

In May 2011, Scotland Yard launched its own investigation of Madeleine's disappearance, assigning a team of 29 police officers to the case, along with eight civilian consultants. Scotland Yard investigators eventually settled on the theory that Madeleine had been taken during a burglary gone wrong. Because there had been a rapid increase in the volume of burglaries in that area in the months preceding Madeleine's disappearance (including cases where the burglars had robbed houses on the McCann's block by entering through the window), they theorized that burglars had kidnapped Madeleine after she woke up and saw their faces during the middle of their robbery attempt.

The British investigators also questioned a group of manual laborers who were working out of a white van in that area at the time of Madeleine's disappearance, as well as two convicted child molesters who were reportedly in that general area during that timeframe. However, despite the developments of new leads in the case, British investigators were never able to determine who actually kidnapped Madeleine.

Suspects

Robert Murat

The first suspect identified by Portuguese police was Robert Murat, a British-Portuguese consultant who lived with his mother just 150 yards away from the location where Jane Tanner spotted a man carrying a barefoot child. Three separate members of the McCann's party later stated that they saw Murat near the resort of the evening of May 3rd, although both Murat and his mother told police that he was at home all-evening long.

Police conducted a thorough investigation of Robert Murat and his possessions, going so far as to conduct a forensic analysis on his computer, phone, and video camera, and even searching his home and property with police sniffer dogs and ground-penetrating radar. Despite the police investigation of Murat and his property, he was cleared on July 21, 2008, when the Portuguese justice department closed the case. However, he was questioned again in 2014 by Portuguese police on behalf of Scotland Yard once the case was re-opened.

Gerry and Kate McCann

While Madeleine's parents were initially viewed with sympathy by the media and general public, they soon became suspects in the case. On June 6th, 2007, a German journalist asked the McCanns if they were involved in the daughter's disappearance during a public press conference. Later that month, local Portuguese paper began writing a series of accusatory articles about the McCanns and their role in their daughter's disappearance.

One of the factors that led to so much speculation about the McCanns and their potential role in their daughter's disappearance was the fact that their initial interview with local police was conducted using a translator. The police investigators would ask a question in Portuguese and then have the translator ask the question in English. The McCanns and their friends would then answer the question in English, which was then translated into Portuguese for the police. Finally, the police then typed up the statement provided by the McCanns and members of the Tapas Seven in Portuguese, before verbally reading the statement back to them in English and asking them to sign the document. This constant translation may have contributed to the discrepancies contained in the statements of all those present that night.

There were several inconsistencies in the McCann's statements. For instance, both parents initially said that they entered the apartment through the locked front door when the checked on their children. However, they would later state that they entered the patio doors at the back of the apartment. In addition, the parents alternatively stated that the patio door was both locked and unlocked that night, casting doubt on their statements. Gerry McCann later told a British newspaper that they had used the front door to check on their children earlier in the vacation, but that they started using the patio door because the front door was next to the children's room and woke them up on their bi-hourly check-ins.

The McCanns also provided contradictory statements on the room's exterior shutter. While Kate McCann told police that the shutter was closed when she put the children to bed at 7:00pm, she claimed that the shutter and window were both open when she discovered that Madeleine was missing. Gerry McCann told police that he closed the shutter after discovering that Madeleine was gone. He also said that, after investigating the shutter from outside the apartment, he noticed that it could be opened from outside. However, the local police said that the shutter was incapable of being opened from the outside and that the lack of evidence of forceful entry ruled out the theory that the abductors had entered through the window.

This important detail led the local Policia Judiciaria to concluded that Madeleine had never been abducted and that the McCanns had made up the story to hide some wrongdoing committed by the parents, even theorizing that Madeleine had actually died in an accident and that the McCann had created the abduction story to shield themselves from scrutiny.

After suspicions about Gerry and Kate were made public, two police sniffing dogs were brought in by Mark Harrison, a national search specialist for the British National Policing Improvement Agency, to conduct an investigation of the apartment, as well as items left by the McCanns and their rental car at the time of Madeleine's disappearance. The two dogs were taken throughout the entire resort, including inside of the McCann's apartment; the dogs alerted their handlers that they smelled signs of Madeleine at the apartment, but did not alert their handlers anywhere else in the resort.

Additionally, the dogs also alerted their handlers of a clue directly behind the couch in the apartment, as well as under the veranda of the bedroom that Gerry and Kate were sleeping in at the time of Madeleine's disappearance. Furthermore, upon additional investigation the cadaver dog alerted its handler when walked around the McCann's rental car, particularly around the outside of the car and inside the trunk of the car. However, the Sunday Times would later say that footage of this investigation clearly showed the dog's handler manipulating the dog and encouraging it to signal a find when passing by those locations.

DNA Analysis

On August 8th, 2007, DNA samples from the McCann's rental car were sent to the Forensic Science Service in Birmingham, England, for testing. The low copy number DNA analysis, which is known for its lack of accuracy and inability to draw conclusive results, demonstrated that 15 out of 19 of Madeleine's DNA pieces were found in areas where the cadaver dogs had signified Madeleine had been, both in the apartment and in the McCann's rental car.

Once Portuguese authorities were notified of the results of this DNA test, they officially abandoned the abduction hypothesis and marked Madeleine's parents as official suspects in the case. They even offered the McCanns a plea deal: they would receive a two-year sentence or less if they admitted that Madeleine had died in an accident and that Kate had hidden the body out of fear of being arrested. Gerry McCann cooperated fully with the police and answered all of their questions; however, Kate refused to answer the authority's question on advice from her attorney.

On September 10th, 2007, the head of the local police department signed a report which concluded that Madeleine had died accidentally in the McCann's apartment and that the McCanns had faked an abduction in order to hide their role in their daughter's death.

Conclusion

Despite the views of the Portuguese investigators, as well as the information uncovered by Scotland Yard, it is likely that the truth surrounding Madeleine's disappearance may never be fully known. While the McCanns and members of the Tapas Seven were accused of being involved in Madeleine's disappearance several times over the years, they have repeatedly denied any involvement in the abduction. Furthermore, both the McCanns and several members of the Tapas Seven have won libel suits against news organizations who accused them of being involved in Madeleine's disappearance.